Henry Richard

Evidences of Turkish Misrule

Henry Richard

Evidences of Turkish Misrule

ISBN/EAN: 9783743317154

Manufactured in Europe, USA, Canada, Australia, Japa

Cover: Foto ©ninafisch / pixelio.de

Manufactured and distributed by brebook publishing software
(www.brebook.com)

Henry Richard

Evidences of Turkish Misrule

The Eastern Question Association.

PAPERS on THE EASTERN QUESTION.

No. 1.

EVIDENCES OF TURKISH MISRULE.

BY

HENRY RICHARD, M.P.

PUBLISHED FOR THE

EASTERN QUESTION ASSOCIATION,

28, CANADA BUILDING, WESTMINSTER;

BY

CASSELL PETTER & GALPIN,

London, Paris & New York.

⁎ *It is necessary to state, in order to explain some expressions that may occur in the first part of this pamphlet, that nearly all that portion of it relating to the condition of Turkey up to the time of the Crimean War, was first published in the year* 1855.

EVIDENCES OF TURKISH MISRULE.

No greater mistake could be committed than to imagine that the recent atrocities in Bulgaria and other Turkish provinces are isolated and exceptional events. The saddest thing connected with these eruptions of brutal violence is the conviction which forces itself on those who have studied the condition of the country, that they are only symptoms of deep-seated and incurable disorders inherent in the constitution of Turkish rule. The Ottoman Turks have been encamped for more than four centuries in Europe. During that time they have been brought into contact with every form of European civilisation ; but they have remained so obstinately impervious to all the influences brought to bear upon them, that we are at last constrained to the conclusion that they have no capacity for civilisation, or if they have, it has certainly not been yet developed. They can fight desperately enough ; but that is the note of barbarism, not of civilisation. When they cease to fight, they seem to fall into a normal state of sloth, sensuality, and decay. Or if they show any sign of vigour, it is the ruthless oppression, every now and then culminating into massacre, which they practise on those who have the misery to be placed in their power.

The country they occupy is suffering from every species of misrule with which a country can be afflicted. Over many a wide expanse the soil, though naturally the richest and most fertile on the face of the earth, lies waste and desolate. All means of material improvement—roads, bridges, mines, docks, harbours—are utterly neglected. Taxation is levied in forms as grinding and oppressive as the utmost ingenuity of cupidity and fanaticism can devise. What is ironically called the administration of justice is itself a mere instrument of extortion and torture. All efforts of the population to rise in intelligence, industry, and wealth are sternly repressed, and whatever progress they make is made in spite of their rulers. The spectacle which Volney saw, and so vividly depicted ninety years ago, still remains. Speaking of Asiatic Turkey, he said : " Everywhere I saw only tyranny and misery, robbery and devastation. I found daily on my route abandoned fields, deserted villages, cities in ruin. . . . . I recalled those ancient ages when twenty famous nations existed in these countries. . . . . This Syria, said I, now almost unpeopled, could then count a hundred powerful cities ; its fields were covered with towns, villages, hamlets. Everywhere appeared cultivated fields, frequented roads, crowded habitations. . . . . What has become of those ages of abundance and of life? . . . . Where are those labourers, those harvests, those flocks, and that crowd of living beings that then covered the face of the earth? Alas! I have surveyed this savage land, I have visited the places which were the theatre of so much splendour, and have seen only solitude and desertion. The temples are crumbled down ; the palaces are overthrown ; the ports are filled up ; the cities are destroyed ; the earth, stripped of its inhabitants, is only a desolate place of tombs."

How is the representation we have given of the state of Turkey proved? By the evidence of a great cloud of witnesses, who have visited the country and have been acquainted with its internal condition for the last fifty years. Among them are men of various nations, of all characters and classes—ambassadors, consuls, travellers, merchants, missionaries, engineers, &c. Their concurrence of testimony affords overwhelming proof that in every respect the rule of the Turks has been a blight and a curse to all the lands over which that rule extends.

This is owing to no want of effort on the part of other Powers, or of promises on their part. Every kind of influence has been brought to bear upon them to induce them to amend their ways—persuasion, remonstrance, menace, friendly aid in the management of their affairs, armed intervention, bloody and desolating wars. These means have indeed elicited from time to time abundant proclamations of good-will and generous intentions, and even of solemn engagements in the form of irades, hatti-i-sheriffs, and hatti-i-humaïons. But after a century's experience Christian nations are obliged to say—

> " They patler with us in a double sense :
> They keep the word of promise to our ear,
> And break it to our hope."

It would be easy to multiply tenfold the evidence given in the ensuing pages. With the rarest possible exception every traveller who visits Turkey bears the same witness.

OPINIONS OF TRAVELLERS AND OTHERS ON THE STATE OF TURKEY.

And first of all, let us give a series of *opinions*, founded upon personal observation, pronounced by travellers who have visited the Ottoman dominions, as to whether that country is in a state of progress or decay. We will begin with M. de Lamartine, who, though in some respects an extravagant admirer and eulogist of the Turkish character, was compelled by what he observed during his travels in the East to come to the following conclusion :—

"The Turks, by the inherent and irreclaimable viciousness of their administration and of their habits, are incapable of governing their present territory in Europe and Asia, or either of them. They have depopulated the countries which owned their sway, and have destroyed themselves by the slow suicide of their government."—*Travels in the East*, p. 752.

And in the year 1834, during a debate in the French Chamber of Deputies, he repeated the same opinion in terms still more emphatic:—

"The Ottoman empire is no empire at all ; it is a misshapen agglomeration of different races without cohesion between them, with mingled interests, without a language, without laws, without religion, without unity or stability of power. You see the breath of life which animated it—namely, religious fanaticism—is extinct. You see that its fatal and blinded administration has devoured the race of conquerors; *and that Turkey is perishing for want of Turks.*"

Mr. J. L. Stephens, the American traveller, who was in that region in 1835, describes the city of Constantinople in these words :—

"We float around the walls of the seraglio, enter the Golden Horn, and before us, with its thousand mosques, and its myriad of minarets, their golden points glittering in the sun, is the Roman city of Constantinople, the Thracian Byzantium, the Stamboul of the Turks; the city which more than all others excites the imagination and interests the feelings; once dividing with Rome the empire of the world ; built by a Christian emperor, and consecrated as a Christian city ; 'a burning and a shining light' in a season of universal darkness, all at once lost to the civilised world, falling into the hands of a strange and fanatical people, the gloomy followers of a successful soldier; a city which for nearly four centuries has sat with its gates closed in sullen distrust and haughty defiance of strangers; which once sent forth large and terrible armies, burning, slaying, and destroying, shaking the hearts of princes and people— *now lying, like a sullen giant, huge, unwieldly, and helpless, ready to fall into the hands of the first invader, and dragging out a precarious and ignoble existence, but by the mercy or policy of the great Christian Powers.*"—*Incidents of Travels in Turkey*, p. 54.

We will take next the opinion of Mr. Eliot Warburton, as able and accomplished a man as ever visited the East :—

"Sultan Mahmoud was one of the five great men who have been the instruments of signalising our age. He ventured on the glorious attempt which few have survived, and none have ever lived to see accomplished—that of regenerating a corrupt people. *The attempt failed utterly, as regarded the creation of new powers and capacities : the old were destroyed, but there was no reproductive principle in the Turkish character.* . . . . They are a gallant people yet, those Osmanlis; and, though they feel that their empire is drawing to a close, and are prepared for the fulfilment of one of those strange old prophecies, like that which prepared the Yncas for the subjugation of *their* country, they will doubtless die fearlessly in defence of those walls so fearlessly won by their fierce ancestors."—*Crescent and the Cross*, p. 390.

Mr. White, in his "Three Years in Constantinople," after showing the utter failure of the Gul Hana edict, which initiated the reform, adverts to the proposal advanced by some to preserve Turkey from utter decay, by raising the different races of which the empire consists into an equality of political privileges with the dominant race, and thus replies to it :—

"But when commerce, industry, intelligence, knowledge, activity, rapidly augmenting population—in short, all the ingredients and incentives to progress and liberty, are on one side, and when comparative ignorance, prejudice, apathy, aversion to speculation and foreign trade, with stationary population, are the characteristics of the other, it is fair to argue that many years would not elapse before the progressing factions would take the lead, and rulers and ruled would change places."

Dr. Aiton, who in 1853 described himself as having "so lately traversed the empire South and North," states it as his opinion, "that Turkey is not worth the preserving, and it were impossible for the two Western Powers to preserve it, were it even worth while." He then quotes the conflicting views expressed by Mr. Cobden and Lord Palmerston in the House of Commons, and adds :—

"We differ entirely from the sentiments of Lord Palmerston, and, as a traveller not long returned from Turkey, we give our testimony decidedly in favour of Mr. Cobden's statement as being nearer the truth."—*The Drying up of the Euphrates, or the Downfall of Turkey*, by John Aiton, D.D., p. 56.

Mr. Fowler, in his "History of the Ottoman Empire," published more than twenty years ago, says :—

"The ejection of the Turk from Europe is now becoming a most desirable event—and even a little farther, perhaps, than Europe would ultimately prove beneficial ; but he may have a chance of reformation in Asia, if he is susceptible of it, though *many regard him as an exhausted specimen of humanity.*"

Mr. Walsh says :—

" There is more of human life wasted and less supplied (in Turkey) than in any other country. . . . . *We see every day life going out in the fairest portion of Europe, and the human race threatened with extinction in a soil and climate capable of supporting the most abundant population.*"—*Kings of the East*, pp. 2—11.

The Rev. Archibald Boyd repeats the same melancholy tale :—

" Altogether decay seems to have written herself in characters so legible upon Turks and Turkey, upon natures and institutions, as to suggest the conclusion *that such a people cannot be expected long to maintain a national existence,* and, perhaps, to force upon the mind the question, whether it be for the interests of humanity and civilisation that they should be allowed to retain possessions which are clearly misplaced in their hands."

And lastly, under this head, we give the opinion of Mr. Thackeray :—

"The Government of the Ottoman Porte seems to be as rotten, as wrinkled, and as feeble as the old eunuch I saw crawling about it in the sun." —*Notes of a Journey from Cornhill to Grand Cairo.*

Then take the opinions of some distinguished European statesmen. The Earl of Clarendon, writing to Lord Stratford de Redcliffe, our ambassador at Constantinople, February 25, 1853, requests him to say to the Sultan :—

" The accumulated grievances of foreign nations, which the Porte is unable or unwilling to redress, the mal-administration of its own affairs, and the increasing weakness of executive power in Turkey, have caused the allies of the Porte latterly to assume a tone alike novel and alarming, and which, if persevered in, may lead to a general revolt among the Christian subjects of the Porte, and prove fatal to the independence and integrity of the empire—a catastrophe that would be deeply deplored by Her Majesty's Government, but which it is their duty to represent to the Porte, is considered probable and impending by some of the great European Powers."

*　　*　　*　　*　　*

" *Nor will you disguise from the Sultan and his Ministers that perseverance in their present course must end in alienating the sympathies of the British nation, and making it impossible for Her Majesty's Government to shelter them from the impending danger, or to overlook the exigencies of Christendom, exposed to the natural consequences of their unwise policy and reckless mal-administration.*"

Lord Stratford de Redcliffe, in a speech delivered at a banquet given to him at Constantinople in 1852, deplores " *the corruption which eats into the very foundations of society, and a combination of force, fraud, and intrigue which obstruct the march of progress, and poison the very atmosphere in which they prevail.*" And again he refers, with profound grief, "to the signs of weakness and error which surround him, to the financial embarrassments of the Government, and the great charter issued by the present Sultan being discredited by the non-execution of its promises."

M. Guizot says :—

"Christian Europe has reason to desire that no private ambition may hasten the downfall of those dilapidated Mussulman states that are languishing and falling into ruin at her gates. . . . Providence, however, has issued visible decrees, and we have a right to be pre-conscious of these, and to hold ourselves in readiness to acknowledge them. The Turks will go out of Europe. The Christian faith and Christian civilisation will not give up their expansive energy. . . . It is an act of prudence as well as of moral sense for all Christian states to pay great regard to this in their policy, and not to place themselves in direct and permanent conflict with facts which will infallibly one day come to pass, and which, when they do come to pass, will be a triumph for humanity."—*Guizot's " Life of Peel,"* p. 162.

M. de Tocqueville, writing to Mr. Senior, says :—

"What say you of our friends the Turks? Was it worth while to spend so much money and to shed so much blood in order to retain in Europe savages who are ill disguised as civilised men?"—*Life*, vol. ii., p. 414.

THE MATERIAL CONDITION OF TURKEY.

In regard to the internal condition of the country, its progress in agriculture and commerce, its means of communication, the state of civilisation, social security and comfort enjoyed by the inhabitants— what is the impression produced on the minds of impartial and intelligent observers by the present aspect of Turkey? After con- sulting all the most recent travellers to whose works we could gain access, we are constrained to come to the same conclusion as a writer in the *Edinburgh Review* in 1854, who says :—

"Amidst all its pretensions to reform, every dispassionate observer of the state of the Turkish empire brings back fresh evidence of its decay ; and even those sanguine Orientalists who speak of its progress cannot deny that the population of the Turkish race is rapidly declining—that the most fertile regions of the Old World are smitten with the curse of barrenness under their rule—that the cessation of the fierce and brutal control once exercised over the country by the Sultans has only secured greater impunity to corruption, and that the internal condition of the Government and the empire is one of hopeless confusion. . . . . Never was a state so instructed in the infancy of its civilisation, or so nursed in the decrepitude of its age ; and we owe the innumerable productions which load our table on the subject to the experience of a vast number of persons engaged in these meritorious efforts. *It is remarkable that not one of them in whose veracity and independence confidence can be placed ventures to boast of his success.*"

But as we are anxious to let our readers judge for themselves, we subjoin a series of extracts from various travellers who have visited the country. We begin with Mr. Spencer, who, about the year 1848, passed through all the provinces of European Turkey, and whose competency to form a judgment no man can doubt who has read his very able and interesting work. Were we to cite all the illustrations he furnishes of the decaying and deplorable condition of the country, we should have to transcribe a large proportion of the two goodly volumes before us.

Adverting to a few patches of cultivation he had witnessed in passing through one part of Macedonia, he says :—

"These indications of agricultural industry are never met with except in the vicinity of a village, and these are few and far between ; for this fine plain, so fertile and productive, is very thinly inhabited, being for the most part covered with rank grass, prickly shrubs, and forests of thistles, often attaining a height of seven feet. We also met a number of small lakes and stagnant marshes, caused by the overflowing of the rivers, sending forth their noxious vapours, and producing those intermittent fevers so fatal to the inhabitants of this part of Macedonia—an evil which could easily be obviated by removing the accumulation of sand-banks that bar the passage of the waters through a plain with so inconsiderable a descent to the sea ; but here, as elsewhere in these provinces, the Turkish Government exhibits the most supine indifference in everything that concerns its own interests, and the millions of human beings committed to its charge. We have already said that there are no roads ; a bridge is seldom met with, and when it is, frequently so out of repair that we preferred swimming our horses over the river to crossing it.

"It avails nothing to the general prosperity of a country to possess fine seas, navigable rivers, rich mines, a fertile soil, salubrious climate, and every material for the creation of industrious wealth—all of which the Osmanli has in these provinces. There must be the means of bringing these resources into action by safe and easy means of internal communication, otherwise the country must continue to remain a *terra incognita,* and its inhabitants sink still lower in the slough of barbarism. . . . Yet if we expatiate on these advantages to an Osmanli, whose narrow mind refuses to advance beyond the narrow circle of his forefathers, he will tell you that the empire has prospered, and still prospers, without the introduction of such unnecessary Frank innovations as carriage roads, bridges and canals, which could have no other effect than to facilitate an invasion of their old enemies, the Russians and the Austrians."— Vol. ii., pp. 47, 48.

In describing his journey through Thrace, adverting to the rare spectacle of "seemingly well-cultivated estates" belonging to one Bey, he says :—

"A welcome sight to the traveller in these provinces, *who may travel from sea to sea, from the Danube to Constantinople, without beholding the slightest mark of improvement either in the aspect of the country or the industry of the inhabitants.* About ten years ago, I traversed nearly the same route from Constantinople to the Danube. The country was without roads, as it is now, and several of the bridges that then existed have been carried away by the flood, or fallen from decay, without either the inhabitants or the Government attempting to replace them. . . . It is not alone the absence of any change for the better that so forcibly arrests the attention of the traveller, as the deep settled gloom that characterises country, town, village, people, wherever the Osmanli rules."—Vol. ii., pp. 361–2.

And Mr. Spencer sums up the result of his observations on the whole country in the following emphatic passage :—

"Four centuries have passed away since the Crescent replaced the Cross on the dome of Saint Sophia, and the empire of Constantine crumbled before the might of Othman ; four centuries of ever-increasing intellect, civilisation, and prosperity.

"Nations then semi-barbaric, have not only emerged from the darkness of the middle ages into the full light of the great epoch in which we now live, but their population, as it were, culminating from the very acmé of civilisation, have borne their talent, industry, and energy, to the most distant regions of the habitable world. The wilderness has been cultivated, and the desert peopled; cities have been founded, and railroads laid down in what were, at the period of the Ottoman conquest, the undisturbed solitudes of primæval nature; and nations, great and powerful, have sprung into existence in quarters of the globe then undiscovered. Yet, when the traveller, fresh from the busy scenes of active life, industry, and usefulness, visits the land of the Crescent, expecting to meet with similar evidences of progress and improvement, and seeing none, exclaims : Where are the monuments of the power and the energy of the mighty people who laid the Christian empire of the East in the dust? Where are the proofs that they have for four centuries had dominion over one of the most beautiful and fertile countries in our hemisphere? Where!—the undrained marsh, the sand-choked river, the grass-grown market-place, the deserted field, the crumbling fortress, the broken arch; these re-echo, where! Stagnation, death-like stagnation, has ever characterised the rule of the race of Othman. . . .

"Crushed and degraded below the level of humanity, generation after generation of the unhappy Christians of these provinces of European Turkey have passed away like the leaves of the forest, without leaving a vestige behind to tell that they existed. Unheeded and uncared for by those nations of Europe who were employing every energy to reclaim from his savage state the swarthy son of distant India and Africa, and make him a participator in the blessings of civilisation and revealed religion, forgetful of the shame and reproach that lay at their very threshold; forgetful that while the life-blood of Europe quickened the extremities of the universe, a portion of her very self remained torpid and corpse-like."—Vol. i., p. 2.

Let us next take the testimony of Mr. Crowe on this point, who represents the effects of Turkish rule as being as blighting and pernicious in Asia Minor as in Europe :—

"This Asia Minor is, indeed, the greatest disgrace of the Turk, the chief accusation that raises itself against the Ottoman. It is a land capable of the greatest fertility and production, traversed by numbers of rivers—a blessing so rare in so southern a clime. It abounds in ports and minerals. It commands two seas, lies between north, and south, and west, and offers itself as the great channel of communication between the different parts of the globe. There is no country in the world with so many of the elements and capabilities of prosperity. Yet for centuries it has been a desert, a land of oppressors and poverty, spoliation and torture, the very charnel-house of the human kind, counting ten millions of Turks, who can neither thrive nor live industrious themselves, nor allow others to do so. Talk of Turkey in Europe, and of the state of the Christian *rayahs* under the Turks—they are ten times more happy, and the country some hundred times more prosperous and rich, with the small element of a Christian population, even oppressed by the Turks, than can be found in the land which the Turks may be said to have all to themselves. . . . . . ."—*The Greek and the Turk*, pp. 175, 176.

No less explicit is the language of Mr. Bayle St. John, also a traveller in Turkey, in his work entitled, "The Turks in Europe."

"We have but to cast a glance over the vast provinces which stretch from the banks of the Danube to the limits of constitutional Greece, to see the natural results of the system I have described, carried on by a people so brutal and barbarous as the Turks. These provinces do not contain one quarter of the population they are capable of supporting, and, unlike other countries, the plains are almost desert, whilst the mountains and a few large cities contain the chief part of the inhabitants. Wherever there is a centre of Turkish authority established, a wilderness is at once created around. The greater proportion of the Bulgarian population is dispersed in villages far from the high roads, and a wholesome terror, as I have hinted in a previous chapter, is from time to time struck into them by invasions of armed tax-gatherers. Nothing can be more melancholy than a journey southward from the Danube towards Constantinople. The Bulgarians are naturally a mild and good people, but, as is well known, they have more than once been goaded by excessive oppression into rebellion. . . . . If we traverse the Balkan range, and enter upon the vast plains of Thrace, the deserts become naturally more dismal than ever. We are approaching the capital. Adrianople is surrounded by vast expanses covered with cemeteries, and the whole country between that city and Constantinople seems as if it had been just visited by a pestilence. It consists of a vast undulating plain, entirely denuded of trees, and cut up by numerous streams of water, which were once bordered by flourishing towns and fields. Now and then a miserable hamlet occurs ; but there are places in which during twelve hours of hard marching there is not a house visible, not a tree, not a shrub."—P. 154.

The following is the language of Mr. Fowler on this point :—

"The climate of European Turkey is perhaps superior to that of any other region of Europe ; the seasons succeed each other with great regularity ; the atmosphere is extremely salubrious, and friendly to the human constitution ; but we see this magnificent country, which nearly equals France in extent, and is superior to it in fertility and the variety of its productions, for the most part a desert, and devoid of population. The magnificence of the scenery is occasionally marred by the sight of crumbling towns and villages, the result of the blight of despotism, which, having ground down the labouring agriculturist beyond the power of endurance, he has abandoned to tyranny the soil on which he once located, and is gone to seek another precarious home. . . . . Immense territories in Southern Europe now lie waste that might be gilt every year with luxuriant corn-fields. The barbarous government of Turkey has laid waste some of the richest gardens and corn districts of the old world. Turkey in Europe, if well governed, might be as rich a country as France or Germany. Corn-fields and vineyards might cover its millions of acres, and those very provinces of which Russia has now taken possession would, no doubt, under Russian protection, and regular government, however tyrannical and restrictive, increase their agricultural and commercial wealth to an indefinite extent ; *but so long as they remain under the mal-administration of the Turk, who is neither a farmer nor a man of business, and thinks it beneath the dignity of his character to follow any other profession than that of soldier and tax-gatherer, and who thinks all farmers and merchants only the legitimate prey of agas and pashas, there is no hope of amelioration."—History of the Ottoman Empire,* pp. 298—300.

We will next produce a French witness, M. Blanqui, who was sent by Louis-Philippe on a mission to Bulgaria and Constantinople in 1841, and who published his observations in 1845, in a work entitled "Voyage en Bulgarie":—

"From Adrianople to Constantinople is a distance of about fifty leagues. The vast space between the two cities is entirely destitute of trees, and presents the aspect of a long, wide, undulating plain, traversed by more than thirty watercourses. . . . .

"There is something more tristful in the unparalleled journey between these two capital cities. This is the countless number of cemeteries one finds in places where every sign of human habitation has disappeared. What signify these cemeteries? When were they formed? Why do they exist in their entirety, while one cannot find the slightest trace of the towns and villages which stocked them with so many dead? . . . .

"But there are things even more sad than these cemeteries without villages—I mean villages without inhabitants. I saw a good many such between Adrianople and Constantinople: the houses were open to wind and rain, the roofs had fallen in, the domestic hearth was empty. Lizards, rats, screech-owls, bats, had taken the place of human beings, destroyed by plague or by poverty, or dispersed by emigration; and these villages were surrounded by fertile lands, and everywhere flowed rivulets and brooks, and the sky overhead was pure and serene; and if, now and then, a tree existed near a fountain, it was so grand and so beautiful, that fifty men on horseback might shelter themselves in its shades. *What, then, has transformed these fertile countries of Thrace into desolated steppes? What but Mussulman barbarity? The mosque alone stands erect in the midst of the ruins which it has caused. The only living creatures we saw were birds of prey.* . . . .

"The desert extends to the very ramparts of Constantinople. As we approached the capital we expected to find some sign of road-making; there was none. The Turks have everything *to begin.*"

Another intelligent foreigner, an officer in the Prussian service, Hubert von Boehm, who some years ago visited Turkey, speaks in the following terms:—

"By a system of falsehood and misrepresentation the Porte has succeeded, to some extent, in turning a little of our general attention from the embroiled and incomprehensible affairs of Turkey, and so much the more as during the last few years nearly every country in Europe has been absorbed by its own internal affairs; but the Turkish Government has carried this system of deceit too far for the safety of its integrity. By hastily building up fragile imitations of European institutions without bases, it has given flagrant evidences of its imbecility and enervation; and by no means of its striving for civilisation, or awakening to intrinsic new strength, as has been so often and so loudly trumpeted by its *Journal de Constantinople.* . . . .

" Of all the great resources of the Turkish empire, little more has remained than a neglected and thinly-populated land, and a lazy, strengthless population. Richly as nature has endowed the land, man has recklessly turned its gifts into curses. The forests lie waste, the fields uncultivated, and the most fruitful and most beautiful districts, changed into dreary deserts, are no longer able to nourish a tribe of beggars. The rule of the Turks has not built a village nor tilled an acre, nay, hardly planted a tree ; and the often-dreamt-of southern vegetation has hidden itself in some corners of the Bosphorus ! The stranger, who knows Turkey only from historical traditions about her former power and splendour, may well be astonished, on his first visit, at the misery and the ignorance that rule unboundedly over the land.

" But, say the defenders of the Government, the country is in a state of transition ; some of the worst traits of Turkish despotism have disappeared, and it requires only time to remedy all the evils. Alas! Time knows only a sad and comfortless tale to tell of sickness and imbecility; and it requires more than blind fatalism to rescue the land from threatening ruin.

" The robber-like rapacity of former Ottoman governments, and the venality of all state officers, are too well known to require proofs. Thereby a feeling of fear and insecurity was engendered, which soon penetrated all minds in such a manner that the endeavours of every individual were only directed how to hide his own property and to appear poorer than he was.

" At present artifices and disguise are no longer of use ; the misery and the unspeakable filth shown by the great mass are the real expression of the state of things; and the treasures accumulated in former days are in the hands of few. In the face of these undeniable facts the Turkish papers assert that the social and material condition of the country has improved ! In all European papers such untruths find an echo, and even in Constantinople men allow themselves to be deceived by them."

The Earl of Carlisle visited Turkey just before the Crimean war, and his verdict as to the condition of the country is summed up in the following emphatic words :—

" When you leave the partial splendours of the capital and the great state establishments, what is it you find over this broad surface of a land which nature and climate have favoured beyond all others, once the home of all art and all civilisation ? Look yourself,—ask those who live there ;—deserted villages, uncultivated plains, banditti-haunted mountains, torpid laws, a corrupted administration, a disappearing people."—*Diary in Turkish and Greek Waters*, p. 184.

RELIGIOUS LIBERTY IN TURKEY.

Next, let us inquire into the question of religious liberty, and the condition of the *rayahs*, or the Christian population of Turkey. On no subject is there more egregious misconception than on this. It is proclaimed, with the utmost confidence, that the Government of the Porte is a perfect pattern of impartiality and dignified toleration, —that whatever may have been the oppressions practised in times past upon Christians in that empire, all that has long ago given place to the reign of complete religious equality. And on what evidence are these bold assertions made? Why, on the evidence of the *tanzimats*, or decrees, every now and then issued by the Sultan, which command his Mussulman officials everywhere to treat their Christian fellow-subjects with forbearance and kindness, and grant them full liberty in the exercise of their religion. Nothing can sound fairer, certainly, than these proclamations, but the unanimous testimony of travellers proves, that, beyond the walls of Constantinople, they are little more than so much waste paper. "Habits of toleration and decrees of equality," said the *Edinburgh Review* in 1854, are a "dead letter beyond the diameter of the capital; and we venture to affirm that more acts of cruelty and extortion are still perpetrated in the Turkish empire than in all those countries of Europe which habitually inspire us with the strongest commiseration. Within the last ten years, wholesale massacres of Christians have taken place in Asia Minor." And now for the proofs, which unhappily are too abundant.

"With every desire to amend the condition of the rayah, the evil still remains—religious prejudice and caste—to frustrate the intentions of the most just and equitable Government, and must continue, so long as the laws are administered by a fanatic, ignorant Mussulman. The traveller is daily reminded of this in his intercourse with Turk and rayah—in the one he sees an overbearing ignorance, and in the other a humiliating degradation. In obedience to the old Mohammedan laws, a rayah is restricted from using certain colours when he paints his house or decorates his person. He is not permitted to enter a town on horseback, if it is the residence of a Turkish dignitary; should he meet with one during his route, he must descend till he passes, or escape by another direction; the meanest Turk holds the power to send him on an errand, or make him carry a package; if struck by one he dares not resent the injury; and should he by chance meet a Turkish lady, he is not allowed to look at her, since it is possible he may blight her good fortune with the evil eye. It is true the higher class of rayahs, such as merchants and traders, inhabitants of towns, aware of their newly-acquired rights, do not humiliate themselves in the presence of a Mussulman; but the poor rayah of the village and the commune, ignorant of the privileges which have been accorded to him, still obeys, and, like a good Christian, if he is struck on the right cheek turns the left; and should he be sufficiently daring to assert his rights and refuse the homage required by the privileged class, the whip of the oppressor quickly reminds him that his emancipation is nominal so long as the Turk remains in authority."—*Spencer*, i. 244.

Let it be distinctly borne in mind that this intelligent traveller speaks as the result of his own personal observation in every part of European Turkey. In the second volume he returns to the subject in the following terms :—

"Thus, the poor Rayah whose patient industry supports Sultan, Church and State, is robbed of his last para for the benefit of the pasha, the bishop, and a host of *employés*, down to the lowest tchiboukji. Should fair means fail to extract from him the wages of his labour, recourse is had to violence, till nothing remains to him, save the miserable hut in which he lives with his wife and children : these, if possessing personal attractions, are not always safe from wretches who carry a brace of loaded pistols to enforce submission.

" Human endurance can bear no more. The abject rayah asserts the rights of man, and flies to arms; but alas ! his weapons are nothing better than his implements of husbandry, which he can oppose with little effect against powder and ball. The tacticoes and arnouts are called out, cannon is employed to put down the revolt, and while the poor rayah dies courageously in the field, his wife and children are frequently consumed among the embers of their cabin—the victims of Turkish misrule. Such was the state of a large district in Bulgaria, the extensive pachalic of Widdin, when I arrived at Sophia in 1850.

" The inhabitants of Western Europe have probably heard of the insurrection of Bulgaria, but they cannot entertain the remotest idea of the horrors that accompanied it; and although, thank Heaven ! I was spared the misery of witnessing the contest, the smoking villages that I saw during my route to the Danube, the blackened bones of the inmates, the number of dead bodies that still lay about in defiles and gorges, preyed upon by wolves and half-wild dogs, told a fearful tale of bitter animosity, and how desperate had been the struggle. When it was too late, the Turkish Government ordered an inquiry to be made as to the cause ; but we presume as Zia Pasha, the author of all this misery and bloodshed, had not politically offended, and was known to be favourable to the views of the Sultan, and an enemy of the anti-reform party, no severer punishment was awarded than a reprimand, and to be deprived of his pachalic.

" The Bulgarians have neither the bold determination of their neighbours, the Servians, nor the spirit of enterprise, combination, and fiery valour of the Greeks ; they more resemble the moujik (serf) of Russia—a machine to be guided at the will of a clever engineer. In Upper Moesia, and on the banks of the Morava, where they amalgamate with the Servians, and their own Haiducs of the mountains, and in Thrace and Macedonia, where they come in contact with their neighbours, the Greeks, we find them a totally different people ; but here in Old Bulgaria, where they number three millions, they may be compared to a carcass to be preyed upon by eighty thousand Mussulman vultures—that being the number of Turks residing in the towns on the Danube and the Black Sea. Even to this day—notwithstanding the edict of the Sultan, granting them social rights, and abrogating the ancient laws, which compelled the rayah of every rank, except the clergy, to humble himself in the presence of the elect of Mahomet—a Bulgarian, when he enters the hall of audience of a pasha, or a simple aien, is seen crawling on his knees, and bending his neck in abject submission to the man in power. While travelling, he dismounts from his horse till the great man passes ; and in all the small towns and villages the whole population bend like a reed at the nod of the meanest Turk."—*Spencer*, vol. ii.

Mr. Crowe, it will be seen by the subjoined extract, declares that even in Constantinople, and under the very shadow of the embassies of the great Western Powers, the old fanatical hatred of Christians was most oppressively manifest :—

"The first feeling of the Frank, when he finds himself in the streets of Constantinople, or even of Pera, is one of humiliation. He has just quitted his abode on a vessel where he was treated with respect, and if he came by land, his firman and expenditure will have saved him from being jostled and insulted by those around him. But once in the streets of Constantinople, the Frank cannot be mistaken in perceiving that he is surrounded by a crowd of barbarians, filthy fanatics, and ferocious ruffians, who regard him with ineffable yet undisguised contempt. The looks of the fellows sufficiently express this; but a very trifling accident, any collision with you or your dragoman, unless the latter be an official Kawas, will call upon your Christian head, and upon those of your relations, a volley of filthy vituperation at which the blood boils. The desire to have this rabble taught their true value and position in the scale of human existence, is the strongest feeling that animates a stranger on first visiting Constantinople. Custom may blunt and politics outweigh susceptibility, as well as the wishes it excites. But however reckless one may become of Turkish execration, and however inimical to the idea of having Russia lording it in the capital of the East, it would afford infinite pleasure to most people to learn that the rabble of Constantinople were kicked into the Bosphorus.

*　*　*　*　*　*　*

"Very little experience will suffice to show the traveller the immense difficulties in the way of the most liberal Turkish minister to elevate the Christian to anything like even fair tolerance. Row up the Golden Horn to visit the old Christian quarter of the Fanar. You will find oppression and forced humiliation stamped upon every house. Even that of the Patriarch, so powerful and so much talked of, is a dingy, diminutive prison, built of stone, indeed, for security, but craving pardon, by its air and its architecture of meanness, for daring to use so costly a material. The little church,—the only church of the Christian within its walls,—is equally begrimed, equally humble. The very population walk with a bowed expression. And this feeling of self-degradation, of which the European cannot divest himself in any part of Constantinople, becomes in the Fanar so painful that one is obliged to rush out of it. In doing so, and emerging from the gates, you enter, unawares perhaps, the Turkish suburb of Eyoub, famous for the mosque in which all the descendants of Mahomet gird them with the sword. If you dare approach that mosque, you will be stoned. You must sneak through the bye-lanes around, and steal a furtive peep. Curiosity more indiscreet might cost you your life."
—*The Greek and the Turk*, pp. 183—9.

The Rev. Horatio Southgate thus describes what he himself witnessed in the streets of Constantinople long after the pretended " Reform " had commenced :—

"On the morning of the paschal, after the public prayer was ended, it belonged to the soldiers to carry back the mats which had served them in their devotions, to the place whence they were taken. Instead, however, of performing the labour themselves, they dispersed through the crowds, and singling out the *rayahs* who happened to be there, compelled them to take the mats upon their shoulders and bear them. I saw one Armenian seized. He was a young man of respectable appearance, and refused when arrested to perform the scandalous task. Immediately some twenty soldiers set upon him, and attempted to beat him into submission. He resisted manfully for a few minutes, while they, standing in a circle round him, kicked him from side to side, like a football. He offered to hire a porter to carry the burden, but they persisted in imposing the contumely upon him, and he walked away under his burden, sobbing with shame and vexation. *We know that the insult was forced upon him because he was a Christian.* I witnessed other scenes of a similar kind during the following days of the festival. *They filled me with the deepest indignation, but the oppression of rayahs became afterwards so familiar a sight to me, that the first effects gradually ceased.* It is only now, when looking back on those scenes from the favoured home of Christianity, that I feel a return of the first glow of indignation, and mourn, as I then sincerely mourned, over the desolate heritage of Zion in the land where she held her earliest and broadest sway."—*Travels in Turkey and Persia*, by Rev. Horatio Southgate, vol. i., pp. 113—14.

The Author of " Eothen " observed the same thing of Damascus.

"Until about a year or two years before the time of my going there, Damascus had kept up so much of the old bigot zeal against Christians, or rather against Europeans, that no one dressed as a Frank could have dared to show himself in the streets ; but the firmness and temper of Mr. Farren, who hoisted his flag in the city as Consul-General for the district, had soon put an end to all intolerance of Englishmen. . . . In the principal streets there is a path for foot-passengers raised a foot or two above the bridle-road. Until the arrival of the British Consul-General, none but a Mussulman had been allowed to walk upon the upper way. Mr. Farren would not, of course, suffer that the humiliation of any such exclusion should be submitted to by an Englishman, and I always walked on the raised path as free and unmolested as if I had been in Pall Mall. The old usage was, however, maintained with as much strictness as ever against the Christian rayahs and Jews. Not one of these could have set his foot on the privileged path without endangering his life. I was walking one day, I remember, along the raised path, 'the path of the faithful,' when a Christian rayah from the bridle-road below saluted me with such earnestness, and craved so anxiously to speak and be spoken to, that he soon brought me to a halt. He had nothing to tell except only the glory and exaltation with which he saw a fellow-Christian stand level with the imperious Mussulmans. . . . His lips only whispered, and that tremulously, but his flashing eyes spoke out their triumph more fiercely : ' I, too, am a Christian ; my foes are the foes of the English. We are all one people, and Christ is our King."—*Eothen*, p. 238.

Dr. Aiton gives his own experience on this point :

"There are three Christians to every Mohammedan in Turkey in Europe. In these circumstances, is it not a strange sight to see this country fighting in the year 1853 for the maintenance of Mohammedanism in Europe ?—the religion of a false prophet—a religion which perpetuates error, slavery, and misery. Much has been said of late as to the extreme toleration of the Turkish authorities and people as to those who differ from them in their religious belief, and also as to their enlightened liberality in Free Trade ; and certainly facts can be adduced in support of their boasting averments striking enough,

B

especially respecting visitors to the garden of Gethsemane, and other places about Jerusalem ; but still it is evident that this feeling is of late and rapid growth, and that it arises more from a consciousness on the part of the Sultan and his Ministers of their dependence on the protection of Christian States than from any inherent principles of their religion or civil polity ; and it is also to be feared, if their present difficulties or dangers were removed, that they would relapse into the barbarities and intolerances of former times. In the large cities, such as Smyrna and Constantinople, the Christians enjoy a certain amount of protection from the *surveillance* which is usually exercised over them ; *but in the main streets of these cities fifty times have the Mussulmans spit at us, merely because we were Nazarenes ;* and in Palestine and other remote provinces we enjoyed the distinction of being stoned and hooted by a rabble of Mohammedans at our heels, merely because we were ' Haji,' *i.e.*, pilgrims."— *The Drying up of the Euphrates*, p. 64.

Similar is Miss Martineau's records of her own experience :—

" At Nablous the bigotry of the people is so great that till of late years no Christian was permitted to set foot within the gates. Ibrahim Pasha punished the place severely, and made the people so desperately afraid of him that they observed his commands pretty much as if he had power in Syria still. One of his commands was, that Christians should not be ill-treated ; so we entered Nablous, and rode through it to our encampment on the other side. *During our passage I had three slaps in the face from millet-stalks and other things thrown at me; and whichever way we looked the people were grinning, thrusting out their tongues, and pretending to spit.*"—*Eastern Life, Present and Past*, p. 529.

Who does not remember the affecting accounts given by Mr. Layard of the horrible and wholesale massacre of the Nestorian Christians by the Kurds, only a short time before his visit to that region? And whether this and similar acts are committed with the connivance of the Turkish Government, or whether they are powerless to restrain the fanaticism of their own subjects, it amounts practically very much to the same thing. A government that is too impotent either to prevent or to punish outrages so gross and revolting upon a whole community of innocent Christian people, is almost as great a curse as if it were itself an active agent in the persecution.

" It was near Lizan," says Mr. Layard, "that occurred one of the most terrible incidents of the massacre, an and active mountaineer offering to lead me to the spot, I followed him up the mountain. Emerging from the gardens, we found ourselves at the foot of an almost perpendicular detritus of loose stones, terminated, about one thousand feet above us, by a wall of lofty rocks. Up this ascent we toiled for above an hour, sometimes clinging to small shrubs, whose roots scarcely reached the scanty soil below, at others crawling on our hands and knees ; crossing the gullies to secure a footing, or carried down by the stones which we put in motion as we advanced. *We soon saw evidences of the slaughter. At first a solitary skull rolling down with the rubbish ; then heaps of blanched bones, further up fragments of rotten garments.*

As we advanced, these remains became more frequent—skeletons, almost entire, still hung to the dwarf shrubs. I was soon compelled to renounce an attempt to count them. As we approached the wall of rock, the declivity became covered with bones, mingled with the long plaited tresses of the women, shreds of discoloured linen and well-worn shoes. There were skulls of all ages, from the child unborn to the toothless old man. We could not avoid treading on the bones as we advanced, and rolling them with the loose stones into the valley below. 'This is nothing,' exclaimed my guide, who observed me gazing with wonder on these miserable heaps; 'they are but the remains of those who were thrown from above, or sought to escape the sword by jumping from the rocks.' "—*Researches in Nineveh*, vol. i.

But Mr. Layard, after narrating these events, led his readers to hope that they were done without the cognizance of the Government, and that when known, the wrongs of the Nestorian Christians would be amply redressed. We believe that he himself represented the matter to the Porte, whose promises, as usual, were prompt and plausible. Officers were sent professedly to inquire into and to punish the atrocities, and to take the Christians under the paternal protection of the Sultan. Well, Mr. Layard paid a second visit to the same region, and this is the description he gives of how the persecuted Nestorians fared under the shadow of their Turkish protectors :—

"Their church was in ruins—around were the charred remains of the burnt cottages, and the neglected orchards overgrown with weeds. A body of Turkish troops had lately visited the village, and had destroyed the little that had been restored since the Kurdish invasion. The same taxes had been collected three times—and even four times over. The relations of those who had run away to escape from these exactions had been compelled to pay for the fugitives. *The chief had been thrown, with his arms tied behind his back, on a heap of burning straw, and compelled to disclose where a little money that had been saved by the villagers had been buried. The priest had been torn from the altar, and beaten before his congregation. Men showed me the marks of torture on their body, and of iron fetters round their limbs. For the sake of wringing a few piastres from this poverty-stricken people, all these deeds of violence had been committed by officers sent by the Porte to protect the Christian subjects of the Sultan, whom they pretended to have released from the misrule of the Kurdish chiefs.*"

Take another passage from the same work :—

"The Nestorian community had greater wrongs to complain of than their Patriarch. The Turkish Government, so far from fulfilling the pledges given to the British embassy, had sent officers to the mountains, who had grievously ill-treated and oppressed the Christian inhabitants. The taxes which the Porte had promised to remit for three years, in consideration of the losses sustained by the unfortunate Nestorians during the massacres, had not been, it is true, levied for that time, but had now been collected altogether, whole districts being thus reduced to the greatest misery and want. Every manner of cruelty and torture had been used to compel the suffering Christians to yield up the little property they had concealed from the rapacity of the Turkish authorities. The pasture and arable lands around their villages had been taken away from them and given to their Kurdish tyrants."

One other witness we shall cite on this part of our subject. Macfarlane, in the Appendix to his volume, gives in detail the facts of that terrible persecution of the Christians, which he describes in general terms in the following extract:—

"I have said elsewhere, and I must here repeat, that Lord Stratford de Redcliffe has been singularly unfortunate in his efforts to protect the Christian element of the population, and to induce the Turks to practise consistently that perfect religious toleration, the merits of which have been so frequently and so loudly claimed by and for Reschid and his partisans. His Lordship (then Sir Stratford) obtained in 1845 a decree full of religious toleration. Every Christian rayah was to have full liberty of conscience and of worship. Those who were Christians in disguise were to declare themselves, and to resort without fear or restraint to their own places of worship. This fine decree led immediately to one of the most frightful of religious persecutions—to multiplied murders, to massacres, to execrable tortures, to expatriation, famine, disease, and nearly every horror that can afflict humanity. And this persecution was not the act of a tumultuary mob—was not the effect of a sudden uncontrollable outburst of popular fanaticism—no, it was the act of the Government; it was directed by pashas, mudirs, and mufties; and to the Government the onus and odium must attach for ever. *I saw the surviving victims, I verified all the facts and circumstances*, and I was most intimately acquainted with the Frank Christians who nobly exerted themselves to put a stop to these Turkish atrocities. I could well enter into the feelings of our Brusa consul and my old friend Donald Sandison when he went to remonstrate with the bloated pasha, who, as usual, received him seated in state on his divan, or broad sofa. After some brief compliment, Mustapha Nouree motioned the consul to take a seat at his side. 'No,' said Donald, with the spirit of a true Highlander; 'No! I will not sit there! your divan is steeped in blood! you are reeking with the blood of Christians.'" —*Doom of Turkey*, p. 224.

THE MORAL AND SOCIAL CONDITION OF TURKEY.

As to the moral and social condition of the Turks, it is such that we can scarcely dare allude to it. By the combined influence of slavery and polygamy their depravity and degradation are unutterable and inconceivable. "These two hellish practices," says Miss Martineau, speaking from what she saw in Egypt, "which, as practices, can clearly never be separated, are here avowedly connected; and in that connection are exalted into a double institution, whose working is such as to make one almost wish that the Nile would rise to cover the tops of the hills and sweep away the whole abomination." We hardly know whether we ought to give the following quotation from Mr. Crowe's work; and yet while some of our countrymen are allowing themselves to be deceived by declamations about the noble character of the Turk, and the marvellous improvements going on in Turkey, we do not feel that we are at liberty to suppress it. As for England taking such a people under its special patronage and protection, we believe the thing would not be tolerated for a moment but for the profound ignorance which prevails as to their habits and condition.

"The question that naturally arises here is, What becomes of the female progeny of the poor in Constantinople? To this one is sorry to have to reply that the very poor in Constantinople have no progeny, because they can have no women. We know not exactly the number of females in the Turkish capital, which makes up a population of seven or eight hundred thousand; but the number, whatever it is, is very unfairly and unnaturally divided ; for whilst the harem of the rich teems with women, there are none in the lowest classes of the population, and but few even in the class above it. A wife is expensive in any country, but in Turkey more than anywhere else, inasmuch as a Turkish wife is not fit for or capable of labour of any kind. She could not sweep a room, she durst not go to market. She must have a slave to perform those menial offices. And there is besides the expense of decorating, covering, and immuring a wife—another necessity of Mohammedanism. No labouring man, then—not even an artisan—can afford a wife. What is the consequence? Concubinage? But there are no women. I will not pursue this subject into any more of its horrid developments, further than to observe that the lower orders of a Turkish city do not reproduce their kind —they die out on dunghills."—*The Greek and the Turk*, pp. 208—9.

Under such arrangements as these, the Turkish population is slowly but certainly diminishing. And to hasten on the process, we are told that among the higher classes infanticide is a common practice. Thackeray, describing what he saw at the Mausoleum of the late Sultan Mahmoud's family in Constantinople, has this passage, relating to a fact which is notorious enough, and which serves to illustrate a custom equally notorious, which has prevailed for centuries and still prevails, in "the liberal and enlightened Government of the Porte."

"In this dismal but splendid museum I remarked two little tombs, with little red fezzes, very small and for very young heads evidently, which were lying under the little embroidered palls of state ; I forget whether they had candles too ; but their little flame of life was soon extinguished, and there was no need of many pounds of wax to typify it. These were the tombs of Mahmoud's grandsons, nephews of the present light of the universe, and children of his sister, the wife of Halil Pacha. Little children die in all ways; those of the 'much maligned' Mahomedan royal race perish by the bow-string. Sultan Mahmoud (may he rest in glory!) strangled the one; but, having some spark of human feeling, was so moved by the wretchedness and agony of the poor bereaved mother, his daughter, that his royal heart relented towards her, and he promised that should she ever have another child it should be allowed to live. He died, and Abdul Medjid (may his name be blessed !), the debauched young man whom we just saw riding to the mosque, succeeded. This sister, whom he is said to have loved, became again a mother, and had a son ; but she relied upon her father's word and her august brother's love, and hoped that this little one should be spared. The same accursed hand tore this infant out of its mother's bosom and killed it. The poor woman's heart broke outright : at this second calamity she died. But on her death-bed she sent for her brother, rebuked him as a perjurer and an assassin, and expired, calling down the Divine justice on his head. She lies now by the side of the two little fezzes :—

* * * * * * * *
* * * * * * * *

"After the murder of that little child, it seems to me one can never look with anything but horror upon the butcherly Herod who ordered it. The death of the seventy thousand Janissaries ascends to historic dignity, and takes rank as war. But a great prince and light of the universe, who procures abortions, and throttles little babies, dwindles away into such a frightful insignificance of crime, that those may respect him who will. I pity their excellencies the ambassadors who are obliged to smirk and cringe to such a rascal."

As to the effect of such a moral and domestic system as prevails among the Turks on the training of children, and the formation of human character, Mr. Crowe says :—

"The moral and intellectual degradation of the male, is the necessary consequence of the degradation of his natural partner. The seclusion and isolation of one sex, leads to the seclusion and isolation of the individuals of the other. The amenities and attractions of society are gone. In camp alone do men congregate, and when the Turks did so, they certainly developed and retained certain of the heroic virtues, stained by the baseness and cruelty into which military heroism so easily degenerates. Reared by an animal mother, the Turk grows up a young animal, and no more ; with strong fighting propensities and strong sensual ones, and a religion which, checking none of them, merely teaches that immortality was to be gained by that indulgence in lust and in blood, which is the strongest of human passions. Such an animal—we can scarcely dignify him by the name of man—had need of no intellectual development or cultivation, and he had none."—Pp. 201—2.

After all this evidence we may well say, in the words of Mr. M'Culloch, in his *Geographical Dictionary* :—

"Such is the Government which the great Powers of Christendom, including, we are sorry to say, England, profess themselves desirous to maintain in all its integrity ! We hardly, however, think that it is destined to a much longer endurance ; and, happily, into whatever hands it may fall, there cannot be so much as the shadow of a doubt that the overthrow of the Turkish Government and power will be productive of the greatest possible advantage to the interests of humanity."

But before closing what we have to say under this head, we must give a few extracts from the reports of our own consuls in various parts of Turkey, in 1853—4, at the very time when our armaments were in that country, to maintain its Government.

Consul Saunders, under date of Prevesa, April 13th, 1853, writes:—

"The rural population, oppressed by fiscal exactions, and subjected to intolerable acts of violence and injustice, cannot be expected to entertain any but the most rancorous feelings towards their persecutors. The inhabitants of the greater part of these villages being, moreover, exclusively Christians, and seeing no other prospect of relief open to them, are continually thronging the foreign Consulates with a view to seek some friendly intervention."—Part i., p. 378.

Vice-Consul Baratti writes, Scutari, June 1st, 1853:—

"All the desperate characters have raised their heads again, and acts of rapine and robbery are very frequent at the expense of the Christians. *Omar Fasha, the Governor of this province, is a Mussulman, and sees with perfect inaifference all these excesses.* The Christians, who are exposed to the vengeance ot their enemies, live in a continual state of alarm."—P. 379.

Consul Neale writes, Turnour, June 28th, 1853—

That "the Christian population of Bulgaria are opposed to any foreign occupation," and that, "were it not for the recurrence of these wanton and cold-blooded murders, and the consequent total insecurity of life, the Bulgarians would ask for arms to resist an invasion of the country."—P. 381.

The following is an extract from a Proclamation of the Christian subjects of the Porte in Epirus, in March, 1854 :—

"The cruel bondage under which we, the population of Grecian Epirus, have laboured for upwards of four centuries, is not unknown to the Sovereigns and people of Christendom. Tyrannical fury has spared neither life nor property, nor left us any kind of liberty. God created us men in His own image and similitude ; whereas we are treated as beasts. The temples of our ancestral faith have been a thousand times impiously polluted and despoiled ; the graves of our fathers opened, and their bones frequently cast into the fire ; the honour of our wives and children continually outraged ; so that our breath alone remains to us, and that but to augment our sufferings. Our voice and language only avail us to appeal and protest against such impious acts of the infidels ; latterly, since the differences on the Russo-Turkish question, the oppressions towards us Christians have been multiplied. Cumulated oppressions, insults, and dishonour, sacrifice of life without end, spoliation upon spoliation, and all the direful woes of Hades itself, are written in our book of life."—*Correspondence respecting the Relations between Greece and Turkey*, p. 61.

Here are some further extracts from the letters of Consul Saunders, March, 1854 :—

"Among other cases brought forward was one where a mother had her son and daughter bound before her eyes and menaced with frightful tortures, boiling oil being prepared to pour upon them for this purpose, unless a large sum of money, which the family was supposed to possess, were immediately consigned ; while the unfortunate mother, producing every species of valuable which she could collect, was with difficulty enabled to satisfy the rapacity of these ruffians, who eventually decamped with a large booty. It should be observed that the parties concerned in the outrages are mostly wealthy Mussulman proprietors, who scruple not to commit every species of atrocity on such occasions."—P. 127.

" From the details so obtained, I learn that the town of Paramithia, and a considerable number of Christian villages of that and the adjacent districts, have been plundered, and in many instances burnt to the ground, by the Mussulman Albanians, under the command of certain chiefs, whose names are known ; that churches and monasteries have been pillaged and laid waste ; women and children carried away captive ; a vast amount of cattle and other property conveyed to distant parts ; and many individuals, particularly old men, helpless infants, and females, tortured and slain in a manner too brutal to describe."—P. 152.

In the year 1854 Sir Culling Eardley published a pamphlet,* which proves that the law which dooms a Mussulman converted to Christianity to summary death, was in force at that very time in Turkey, whatever professions and promises may have been made to the contrary. "I believe it to be a fact of history," says Sir Culling, "that a Mussulman, who avowed himself a believer in Christ at Adrianople, was actually put to death in 1853." Well may he add, "It is an odious and unchristian inconsistency, that while Christendom is sustaining the Government of Turkey, the Government of Turkey should be suffered to decapitate Mussulmen for becoming Christians." "We cannot conceal from ourselves the fact," says the Rev. G. Fisch, a Protestant pastor at Lyons, "that this perfidious system of persecution, which only gives a Mussulman who has become a Christian three days to prepare for death, is marvellously calculated to paralyse all missionary effort. . . . . What more strange than to see the Turkish empire, vanquished by our civilisation, and obliged to lean on us in its decay, and yet at the same time making that very Christianity which prevents its downfall a capital crime in any Mussulman who embraces it." Well might Lord Carlisle say, "that some plausible and even some substantial grounds might be alleged for the propositions of Prince Menschikoff, for," adds his lordship, "I DO NOT THINK IT WELL FOR ANY CHRISTIAN STATE TO LEAVE ITS CO-RELIGIONISTS TO THE UNCOVENANTED FORBEARANCE OF MUSSULMAN RULERS."

STATE OF TURKEY SINCE THE CRIMEAN WAR.

Such was the state of things at the time of the Crimean War. That war was expected by sanguine people to be a great turning-point in the history of Turkey. Closer intercourse with the Western nations was to mitigate, if not to remove, the old Mohammedan pre-

* "Christianity in Turkey," pp. 39—44.

judices. Gratitude for the services rendered to them in their extreme need was to dispose the Turks to listen with favour to all the suggestions that might come from their allies for internal reforms in their administration, and especially for a more lenient treatment of their Christian fellow-subjects. The country was to be regenerated by an infusion of the elements of Western civilisation. To this end Turkey was admitted, for the first time, into the concert of European nations. England and France became sponsors for its financial solvency. The firman elicited from the Sultan at the time of the Treaty of 1856 was proclaimed as the Magna Charta of Turkish freedom.

It now remains to be seen how far these hopes have been realised. And first let us see what was going on at the very time when Christian Europe was fighting the battles of Turkey.

Here is a description, by an eye-witness, of the way in which the Turks treated our poor wounded soldiers, who had been shedding their blood to maintain the independence and integrity of the Ottoman empire. It is from a little book entitled " Experiences of an English Sister of Mercy," published in 1863 :—

"Having access to windows commanding two wharves, we often saw the sick and wounded from Balaclava brought on shore. This was indeed a piteous spectacle—a long file of stretchers, each with a gaunt soldier, clothed in his tattered grey coat, lying helpless (and very often senseless) upon it, being borne by noisy, careless Turks, who really appeared to resort to little expedients in order to increase the sufferings of the soldier ; such as placing the taller of the four bearers at the feet rather than the head ; when about to rest, allowing the framework to fall with a jerk ; or lifting it up unevenly, and thus rolling off the bleeding burden. On one occasion a wounded man was brought in, and two of the bearers had rested their poles on the ground while the other two still retained theirs, thus causing the patient to lie on his head and shoulders. On releasing him we found that he had fainted : a few moments longer would probably have placed him beyond recovery. On another occasion the Turkish bearers, while jesting among themselves, threw a sick man off the stretcher, cutting his face, and giving him a severe shock. When able to speak, his first words were, ' Those frightful men have murdered me.' He did not live long after, though the fall would not have killed a man in health."

No wonder that a distinguished officer in the Crimea, writing home in 1854, should have said :—

" Half of us do not know what we are fighting for, and the other half only pray that we may not be fighting for the Turks."—*Bright's Speeches*, vol. i., p. 473.

To the same effect is the testimony of Mrs. Hornby in letters written from Constantinople in 1856, and published in a work entitled " In and about Stamboul," as to the feelings of the Turks towards their Christian allies after the war was over :—

"It is very dispiriting to discover whàt a people these really are after all they have cost us. As to gratitude, they detest us all the more for the humiliation of obligation. It is all very fine to talk of 'alliance' in the news-papers, or at public dinners, champagne in hand, and with the Crescent and Cross twining affectionately round the English standard and the lilies of France. Depend upon it that only from the most dire necessity will they ever tolerate our interference, and that east and west are not so far divided as our tastes, habits, and every natural tendency."

How was the expectation fulfilled that the Crimean War would soften the prejudices of the Moslems against the Christians, and so open the way for the spread of Christianity in Turkey? Mr. Righter, secretary of the Turkish branch of the Evangelical Alliance at Con-stantinople, writing home towards the end of 1856, says :—

"Now that the foreign troops have been withdrawn, foreign influence seems in a great measure to have declined at the capital, and has entirely ceased in the interior. The *hatti-sheriff* has aroused the bigoted prejudices of the Mussulmans. Violent persecutions have been excited against Protestants both by the Christian sects and Moslems, and there is no protection nor redress. Several aggravated cases have recently been brought before our notice. We have appealed again and again to the European ambassadors, who have interested themselves warmly in the matter, but have been unable to procure any relief to persecuted persons who have been imprisoned or banished."

Dr. Sandwith, in his volume entitled, "Siege of Kars," after referring to a firman published in 1854, promising legal equality before the courts to the Christians, says :—

"Since then I have been nearly two years in the provinces, both in European and Asiatic Turkey, and have seen Christians frequently wronged, but have never heard of their evidence being taken. Each pasha, when questioned concerning this firman, declares he knows nothing of it, no firman of the kind has ever been officially communicated to him ; he must act according to his instructions, he cannot take cognisance of firmans conveyed through European consuls."—Pp. 165—7.

As an example of the way in which the feelings of the Sultan's Christian subjects were rudely trampled on by Mussulman intolerance, he gives the following faithful translation of a *teskéré*, or permit of burial, given by the Cadi of Mardin in the spring of 1855 to a Christian applying for it. He has given and does give, adds Dr. Sandwith, scores of the like kind to all the giaours in his juris-diction.

"We certify to the priests of the Church of Mary, that the impure, putrified, stinking carcase of Saideh, damned this day, may be concealed under ground.   (Sealed)
"El Said Mehurred Faizi.

"A. H. 1271.—Rejib."
(March 29th, 1855.)

One of the first travellers who visited Turkey after the war of 1854—5 was Mr. Nassau W. Senior. He published the result of his observations in a work entitled, "A Journal kept in Turkey and Greece in the Autumn of 1857 and the Beginning of 1858."

Before citing some extracts from Mr. Senior's book, we will present to our readers the following summary of its contents from the *Edinburgh Review* of October, 1859:—

"Mr. Senior's journey to the East was made at a time peculiarly calculated to give interest and value to his observations. The war was just over, in which the armed intervention of the Western Powers had rescued Turkey from the impending peril of Russian invasion. A peace had been signed, which had guaranteed the independence and integrity of the Ottoman dominions, and placed the Sultan within the common security afforded by the public law of Europe. Large concessions, conceived in a tolerant and liberal spirit, had been made to the Christian population by the hatti-i-humayoon of February, 1856. Attempts were not wanting to place the Turkish finances on a better footing—to raise loans—to develop the resources of the country, and to carry on the work of Reform. If ever there was a moment in modern times when hopes of the regeneration of Turkey could reasonably be enter-tained after the efforts and sacrifices Europe had made in her behalf, the autumn of 1857 was that time. Yet the evidence Mr. Senior has collected, and the picture he has drawn, can leave no illusion on the mind of any man who believes the one to be true and the other to be correct. We might quote page after page to demonstrate that all our exertions had only served to rescue the most execrable and contemptible Government in Europe from an external danger, without adding anything to its internal strength or vitality. The fourth point of the articles relating to Turkey in the Treaty of Paris, which was to secure to the Christian subjects of the Porte equality of civil and religious rights in exchange for the guarantee extended to the dominions of the Sultan by the Christian Powers, has remained a dead letter. The condition of the Christian population is in truth unchanged, and nothing has occurred to lessen their ineradicable distrust and hatred of their Mussulman rulers. Turkey in fact exists, as an English merchant settled at Galata observed to Mr. Senior, for two purposes :—First, to act as dog in the manger, and to prevent any Christian Power from possessing a country which she herself, in her present state, is unable to govern or protect ; and, secondly, ¡for the benefit of some fifty or sixty bankers and usurers, and some thirty or forty pashas, who make fortunes out of its spoils."

It is necessary to explain that Mr. Senior, instead of giving his own opinions on the state of things in Turkey, has adopted the plan of recording the conversation of a large number of intelligent persons, principally Europeans who had been long resident in the country, and had enjoyed ample opportunities of forming a judgment upon the matters of which they spoke. In the Preface he says, that "while the reader will find on many points great difference of opinion ; on a few, such as the rapid decline of the Ottoman empire in wealth and in population, the corruption of its officials, and the mischief done to it by diplomatic interference, he will find nearly unanimity." We shall therefore confine our extracts principally to those points on which such remarkable unanimity prevails among all the witnesses, Turks, Armenians, British, French, Germans, and Russians. Here is one specimen :—

" 'What impression does the East produce on you?' said one gentleman to me.

" 'I have had time,' I said, 'only to look at the exterior. I see a capital, the streets of which are impassible to wheels, and scarcely to be traversed on foot ; I see a country without a road ; I see a palace of the Sultan's on every promontory of the Bosphorus ; I see vast tracts of unoccupied land, and more dogs than human beings ; these appearances are not favourable to the Government or the people.'

" 'If you have the misfortune,' he answered, 'as I have had, to live among Turks for between two and three years, your opinions will be still less favourable. In government and religion Turkey is a detritus. All that gave her strength, all that gave her consistency, is gone; what remains is crumbling into powder. The worst parts of her detestable religion—hatred of improvement and hatred of the unbeliever ; the worst parts of her detestable government—violence, extortion, treachery, and fraud—are all that she has retained. Never was there a country that more required to be conquered. Our support merely delays her submission to that violent remedy.'

" 'You think, then,' I said, 'that it must come to that?'

" 'I can see,' he answered, 'no other solution ; the Turk is utterly unimprovable. He hates change, and therefore he hates civilisation ; he hates Europeans, he hates and fears all that they propose. There is not a word in the hatti-i-humayoon that does not disgust, or irritate, or alarm him. Nothing but force will oblige him to give it even the appearance of execution. And what is the value of apparent reforms in a people without an aristocracy, without a middle class, without a public opinion, without the means of communication, without newspapers, without even a post-office; accustomed for four hundred years to plunder and oppress rayahs, and to be oppressed and plundered by sultans, pashas, cadis, and janissaries?' "—Pp. 27—8.

In a conversation with another gentleman Mr. Senior asked :—

" ' Is not the hatti-i-humayoon a real reform ?'

" ' It is waste paper,' he answered. ' So far from acting on it, the Turks cannot even understand it. . . . . It is a year-and-a-half old. You cannot point out a single clause to which any effect has been given.'

" ' In time,' I said, ' some fruit will come.'

" 'No fruit,' said G. H., 'has come of the hatti-sheriff of Gul Hâneh, of which the hatti-i-humayoon is little more than a paraphrase. Unless England and France unite to force real reforms on Turkey, I fear we have only delayed her subjugation by Russia.' "—P. 44.

Of the condition of the Christians, another speaker says :—

" You see nothing here [at Constantinople] of Turkish rule. Here they are restrained by European opinion ; but in the remoter districts, where there is no consul to interfere, the Christians, unless they are numerous enough and bold enough to defend themselves, are treated not merely as slaves, but as slaves whom their masters hate. You may fancy what such a slavery is when the master is a barbarian."

Further on we find this testimony from a fourth witness :—

" He gave a frightful account of the misgovernment of Turkish Armenia. . . . . The amount of tyranny may be inferred from the depopulation. You see vast districts without an inhabitant, in which are the traces of a large and a civilised people, great works for irrigation now in ruins, and constant remains of deserted towns. There is a city near the frontier, with high walls and large stone houses, now absolutely uninhabited ; it had once sixty thousand inhabitants."—Pp. 838—9.

Again, Mr. Senior himself says :—

" I do not believe that the Turks are more idle, wasteful, improvident, and brutal now than they were four hundred years ago. But it is only within the last fifty years that the effects of these qualities have shown themselves fully. When they first swarmed over Asia Minor, Roumelia, and Bulgaria, they seized on a country very populous and of enormous wealth. For three hundred and fifty years they kept on consuming that wealth, and wearing out that population. If a Turk wanted a house or a garden, he turned out a rayah ; if he wanted money, he put a bullet into a handkerchief, tied it into a knot, and sent it to the nearest opulent Greek or Armenian. At last, having lived for three centuries and a half on their capital of things and of man, having reduced that rich and well-peopled country to the desert which you now see it, they find themselves poor. They cannot dig, to beg they are ashamed. They use the most mischievous means to prevent large families ; they kill their female children, the conscription takes off the males, and they disappear. The only memorial of what fifty years ago was a popular Turkish village is a crowded burial-ground now unused.

" As a medical man," said Y., " I, and perhaps *I* only, know what crimes are committed in the Turkish part of Smyrna, which looks so gay and smiling, as its picturesque houses, embosomed in gardens of planes and cypresses, rise up the hill. I avoid as much as I can the Turkish houses, that I may not be cognizant of them. Sometimes it is a young second wife who is poisoned by the older one ; sometimes a female child, whom the father will not bring up ; sometimes a male killed by the mother to spite the father. Infanticide is rather the rule than the exception. No inquiry is made, no notice is taken by the police."—Pp. 211—12.

A friend well acquainted with the whole of Turkey said to Mr. Senior as he was leaving Constantinople, " You are going to Smyrna and to Greece. When you are at Smyrna visit Ephesus ; you will ride through fifty miles of the most fertile soil, blest with the finest climate in the world. You will not see an inhabitant nor a cultivated field. This is Turkey. In Greece or in the Principalities you will find comparative numbers, wealth and population. They have been misgoverned ; they have been the seat of war ; but they have thrown off the Turk."—P. 148.

The moral condition of Turkey is still indescribable. There is abundant evidence of a ,fearful kind, but it cannot be publicly produced. The following letter addressed to the Rev. Earnest Hawkins, 8th January, 1863, and which is in the archives of the Society for the Propagation of the Gospel, indicates what cannot be described :—

"Few of you in England know the real horrors of this country. You will see what I mean when I tell you my intention of getting a number of tracts in Turkish written or lithographed, to be distributed by a Turk on the bridges, &c. The tract is to consist of such passages as the history of Sodom and Gomorrah. What can we hope to do with this people? One Englishman, who has to do with multitudes of them, reckons those who are innocent of this hideous vice at one or two in a hundred. A Turkish teacher told an European that those who are guiltless as to that are two in a thousand.

"Stories of assault *sub dio*, effected or attempted, have come to me one after another. These people must be held together? What is our policy supporting? Some one asked me how to account for this in a people the most moral of all—the English people—that these deepest immoralities should be maintained by their patronage? I replied, they are for the most part quite ignorant or unwilling to believe what they hear. Still, it is a condition of morals which makes khans, and baths, and lonely places dangerous to the unwary. . . .

"Believe me (my authority is the best) it is a question of time ; the decay of the Turkish people is going on rapidly ; their numbers are fast decreasing through vice, disease, neglect, and the conscription."

The Rev. William Denton in his work, "The Christians of Turkey," after referring to the practice of polygamy, infanticide, and the military conscription, as accounting in part for the notorious decline of the Turkish race, goes on to say :—

"But all these combined will not fully account for the fact that the Turks are rapidly becoming extinct. . . . The evil lies far deeper. It is one, however, which cannot be laid bare. The hideous, revolting profligacy of all classes, and almost every individual in every class, is the main cause of the diminution. This is a canker which has eaten into the very vitals of society. It is one, however, which has taken so loathsome a form that no pen dares describe the immoral state of Turkish society. It must be abandoned to vague generalities, for happily the imagination cannot picture the abominations which are fast exterminating the whole Turkish race. . . . I have the evidence now before me of persons at present resident in Turkey, as well as of English officers high in the civil service, whose duties have made them acquainted with the real state of society in Turkey; and in addition to these, I have a voluminous report addressed to me by a distinguished foreigner, formerly a colonel in the Turkish service, and, from the varied offices he has filled in that country, of all men one of the most competent witnesses. I have all this evidence before me, but it is so disgusting and obscene that I dare not make use of it. The satires of Juvenal and Petronius Arbiter are decorous in comparison. Students may remember how rabbinical writers describe the sins of the Ammonites and other inhabitants of the land of Canaan, who for their revolting sins were driven out by the children of Israel. That description gives but a partial picture of what is the present state of Turkish society. The

Cities of the Plain were destroyed for sins which are the common, normal, every-day practice of this people."—Pp. 62—4.

The Events in Damascus and the Lebanon in 1860.

It was not long after the peace of 1856 before Europe and the Christian world were furnished with a terrible practical commentary on the hatti-i-haimaïoun, in which the Sultan "recorded his generous intentions" towards the Christian population of his empire.

In the year 1860 the Russian Government called the attention of the great Powers concerned with itself in the Treaty of 1856 to the alarming condition of the Christian provinces subject to the Porte. Prince Gortschakoff, in a circular note dated April 23rd, 1860, states that unless some means were taken to induce the Turkish executive to exert its authority for the repression of disorder and for the protection of the Christians, some terrible explosion would be inevitable before long. But the policy of suspicion was then in the ascendant. The warning was pooh! poohed! as the mere offspring of Russian intrigue. But in the following July the explosion did indeed take place in the fearful atrocities in Syria, by which a hundred and fifty towns and villages were destroyed, ten thousand people were massacred, seventy thousand reduced to starvation, and property destroyed or plundered to the estimated value of four or five millions sterling. The Druses were the immediate agents in the work of horror, but there is the clearest evidence to prove that the Turkish officials, civil and military, not only did not attempt to repress the wholesale murder and pillage going on under their eyes in the Lebanon and at Damascus—that not only did they connive at them openly and obviously, but that they instigated and encouraged them ; nay, that in some instances they were themselves the active agents in inflicting on the unfortunate Christians the inexpressible horrors which filled all Europe with dismay and indignation.

The terrible story was thus summarised from the Parliamentary documents in a letter from Mr. William Wood, which appeared in the *Times* of August 28, 1876.

On May 22, 1860, Hasbeya, a large Christian town under Mount Hermon, was attacked by the Druses. There was a considerable force of Turkish troops in the place, under the command of Othman Bek :—

"This man" (I quote from Mr. Graham's despatch to Lord Dufferin) "on the day of the attack on Hasbeya, told the Christians that he had been sent to protect them from the Druses, but that they must lay down their arms, otherwise they would incur the displeasure of the Government. They accordingly obeyed, believing that he would keep his word. For 'greater security' he invited them all in the Serai Palace, used as a barrack, and the men, with the women and children, crowded into the building."

The arms were sent off with a mockery of an escort, professedly to Damascus, but, as seems to have been arranged, fell into the hands of the Druses.

"The Christians, meanwhile, penned up in the Serai, with hardly any food and water, were now in a state of great suffering. On the 5th of June they began to feel great alarm, for they saw the harem of the Governor preparing to depart. To the questions of the Christians as to the cause of this movement, only evasive answers were given.

"On the 6th many of the soldiers were seen leaving; then the unfortunate people, when it was too late, saw clearly how treacherously they had been deceived. They rushed into the outer court and entreated to be let out. The signal was given, the gates thrown open, and in rushed the Druses, armed with any weapon they could seize, and then commenced an indiscriminate slaughter of all the males. Some, indeed, made their way through the door to the outer gate, only to be seized by the Turkish soldiery. Nor were these passive only in the transaction. Many Christians whom I have examined have sworn to me that they saw the soldiers themselves taking part in the slaughter; and the subsequent behaviour of these brutal troops to the women was savage in the extreme. From the wounds I have seen both on the living and the dead it would appear that they went to work with the most systematic cruelty—ten, twelve, and fourteen deep cuts on the body of one person is not unfrequent. Some of the wounds show that they were made with blunt instruments. In short, everything was used which came to hand, and, according to the nature of the weapon, hands and limbs were cut off, or brains dashed out, or bodies mangled.

"Of all the men in the Serai, some 40 or 50 only escaped. Women the Druses did not slaughter, nor, for the most part, I believe, ill-use; that was left for Turks and Moslems to do, and they did it.

"Little boys of four and five years old were not safe; these would be seized from the mother and dashed on the ground, or torn to pieces before her face; or, if her grasp was too tight, they would kill it on her lap, and in some cases, to save further trouble, mother and child were cut down together. Many women have assured me that the Turkish soldiers have taken their children one leg in each hand and torn them in two."

At Sidon, on the 1st of June, the Christians were attacked in similar manner by the Bashi-Bazouks and other Moslems :—

"For several days the slaughter continued. No Christian outside the town was in safety. If a man, or a male child, he was cut down; if a woman, she was sure to be brutally ill-used."

The same scene of treachery as at Hasbeya was repeated at Deir-el-Kamar. The inhabitants, hearing of the approach of the Druses, prepared to defend themselves; but the Turkish Governor, who had 700 troops at hand, told them they had nothing to fear if they would deliver up their arms. Accordingly the then defenceless men, women, and children were all crowded together into the Serai, under his protection, on the night of the 20th of June :—

"On the morning of the 21st the Druses collected round the town. One of their leaders came to the Serai and desired to speak with the Governor. A conversation was carried on in a low voice by means of an interpreter, for the Turk did not know Arabic. At last a question was asked to which they heard the Governor give the answer 'Hepsi' ('Ab' in Turkish)—*i.e.*, 'all.' Thereupon the Druse disappeared, but in a few moments the gate was thrown open and in rushed the fiends, cutting down and slaughtering every male, the soldiers co-operating. . . . I have good reason to believe, after a careful comparison of all the accounts, that from 1,100 to 1,200 males actually perished in that one day. . . . I myself can testify that the accounts are not much exaggerated. I travelled over most of the open country before the war was over, and came to Deir-el-Kamar a few days after the massacre. Almost every house was burnt and the streets crowded with dead bodies, most of them stripped and mutilated in every possible way. My road led through the town, and through some of the streets my horse could not even pass, for the bodies were literally piled up. Most of those I examined had many wounds, and in each case was the right hand either entirely or nearly cut off; the poor wretch, in default of weapons, having instinctively raised his arm to parry the blow aimed at him. I saw little children of not more than three or four years old stretched on the ground, and old men with gray beards.

"The pasha reached Deir-el-Kamar the day after the slaughter : a fact 'which he will ever lament and deplore as long as he lives.' That is what he says, so of course it is true. . . . Othman Bek—the same who was at Hasbeya—entered Damascus a few days ago, and received the honours of a conquering hero. Nothing can be more infamous than the conduct of Ahmed Pasha and of all the officials."

So far Mr. Graham (*Syrian Despatches*, No. 2, p. 46).

The horrible occurrences which have been detailed above were to be surpassed in a few days at Damascus. The outbreak, which the Governor, Ahmed Pasha, made not the least attempt to check, occurred on the 9th of July. The whole Christian quarter was ruthlessly plundered and burnt to the ground ; 2,000 dead bodies lay unburied amid the ruins, and 20,000 houseless wanderers, whose only crime was that they were followers of Christ, were left to live on charity and ask for justice at the hands of Europe. The Pasha, whose first duty was to have shown himself at the head of his troops and disperse the robbers, kept within his palace during the whole time of the massacre (he was one of the Turkish generals associated with us in the Crimean War), while his troops, fresh from the shambles of Hasbeya and Deir-el-Kamar, joined the Moslem mob in murdering and pillaging.

The Rev. Dr. Thomson, one of the American missionaries in Syria, the well-known author of "The Land and the Book," in a letter to Sir Culling Eardley appealing for help, says :—

"I have been familiar with six bloody wars in this country during the past twenty-seven years, but they were mere boys' play so far as the atrocity is concerned in comparison with this dismal butchery. I have lately read the entire history of the Moslem occupation of Syria from the beginning, and there is no

C

account which equals the tragedies of Rasheya, Hasbeya, Deir-el-Kamar, and Damascus—not to mention other places made desolate by this ferocious war.

"All the numbers in our appeal are too low (75,000 destitute, 10,000 widows) ; whole districts now known to be destroyed are not included in the estimates of this circular.

"Authentic accounts, official and private, from Damascus last night raised the number of the slaughtered in that city to 5,000. Of course the houseless, homeless victims come nearer 20,000 than 10,000 in Damascus alone."

But there is one fact connected with these events in Syria which is most humiliating to Englishmen, namely, that the authors of those atrocities believed that they were doing acceptable service to our country by their acts. Mr. Cyril Graham, who ventured to pay a visit to the mountain a few weeks after the massacres had taken place, describes an interview which he had with one of the Druse chiefs, whose name, he says, "is mentioned with horror by all the Christians as having been the chief instigator of, and the chief actor in, the massacre of the 11th of June."

"He came to see me," says Mr. Graham, "at the house of the other chief, and a conversation ensued, from which it appeared that they still entertained a belief, in common with most of the Druses, that the English Government must be extremely satisfied with what they had done, for they imagined that any diminution of the number of the Christians will be acceptable to us as weakening the French influence in the country."

Later Testimonies.

We will now proceed to inquire from the evidence of other trustworthy witnesses who have traversed various parts of the Ottoman empire within the last fifteen years, how far the promise of reform has been fulfilled. It matters not what was the character of the travellers, or what was the object of their mission ; whether they visited the country for curiosity and adventure, or for purposes of philanthropy, or commerce, or scientific exploration, their testimony is the same on this point—the deplorable condition of Turkey.

In 1863, Miss Mackenzie and Miss Irby passed through a considerable portion of European Turkey, and have related their observations and experiences in the singularly interesting volume entitled "Travels in the Sclavonic Provinces of Turkey-in-Europe."

This work so abounds with evidence of the oppression and general misrule of the Turkish Government, that it is difficult to make a selection. Early in their work they express the conviction, that "any arrangement which would disencumber the thrifty and well-disposed Bulgarian of the yoke of his present barbarous master would certainly prove a gain to civilisation."

They thus describe the system of taxation :—

" As for the taxation in Turkey, grievances commence at the point where in other countries they are supposed to culminate ; so we say nothing of the injustice to a population of millions that it should have no voice in the dis-posal of its money. Granted that the Bulgarians be ready to give all the Government calls for, and, moreover, to pay for exemption from the army—that is, for being disarmed and held down by Mussulmans—still, the greatest grievance remains, namely, the waste and iniquity wherewith the revenue is raised.

" Hitherto the taxes have been paid in kind, a method which always gives the gatherer much power to extort bribes, since he can refuse to value the pre-sent standing corn until half of it be spoiled. But Turkish tax-farmers do not confine themselves to such dry paths of cheating.

" The following is an instance of what constantly occurs :—Two men agreed to keep a flock between them—the one in summer on the mountains, the other in winter on the plain. The tax-gatherer compels the first to pay for the whole, promising that he will ask nothing of the other ; he then goes to the second, and, with a similar promise, forces him likewise to pay for all. In like manner, the Christian can be compelled to pay twice over for exemption from the army, if the tax-gatherer declare his first receipt forged. . . . . A change of system is being introduced which will supersede payment in kind by payment in money. But it is hard to see how this is to prove beneficial, without such means of transport and security of communication as would enable the peasant to bring his produce to market. At present, while he must sell it in the neighbourhood wherein it abounds, he is taxed at the market value.

" The people declare that the oppression is now worse than before, and that this is one of the many *soi-disant* reforms which tell well on paper, while, unless followed up by other reforms, they prove actually mischievous. We ourselves saw the tax-gatherer swooping down on the villages, accompanied by harpy-flocks of Albanians, armed to the teeth."—Pp. 20, 21.

They cite several instances of Christians being murdered by Mohammedans with perfect impunity, and then add :—

" In this manner murders are committed every day, and so long as the victims are rayahs the authorities take no notice ; but even if they did, the conviction of the assassin is hopeless, for a Christian cannot give evidence in criminal cases. It may be asked, Why do the Christians not resist ? In the first place, they are not, like the Mohammedans, armed ; secondly, the injury of a Mohammedan by a Christian, even in self-defence, or the defence of another, is rigorously punished in Mussulman courts."—P. 76.

In a note the authors subjoin the following :—

" Since writing the above, we have found these and other stories related at length in Mrs. Walker's " Through Macedonia to the Albanian Lakes." She also says, " the Christians of Ochrida complain bitterly of the murders of their co-religionists which have taken place in that neighbourhood within the last three years. No less than thirty lives have been sacrificed, but in no single instance have the assassins been brought to justice (page 211). An American missionary told us that near Eski-Sagra, in Bulgaria, where he was stationed, from seventy to one hundred Christians were killed annually by Mussulmans without inquiry being made."—P. 76.

Of Turkish tolerance take the following illustration : –

"There are three Sclavonic schools in Skopia; two contain sixty scholars between them, and another, which is larger, holds a hundred. The Christians have built a large church apparently unmolested, for which liberty they are possibly indebted to the circumstance that Skopia was at one time a Consular station.

"In districts between this and Nish there are places where the Christians, having received the Sultan's firman permitting them to build a church, have seen it twice thrown down by the neighbouring Mussulmans, and only succeeded in keeping it after the expense and labour necessary to rear it a third time."—P. 140.

Nothing is more painful in this book than the revelations it gives as to the state of abject terror and servility in which the unfortunate Christians are held. After describing their visit to a school at the Monastery of Gratchanitza, these ladies say :—

"Before leaving the schoolroom, we ventured a very earnest remonstrance as to the mode in which the pupils had greeted us. At our entrance they had literally fallen down at our feet, and that with a sort of grovelling action, which, if not revolting, would have been ludicrous. We asked how in the world they came to suppose we should wish to be thus received. Their teacher answered, 'The Turks taught it us; their dignitaries require us Christians to prostrate ourselves before them.' 'But we are not Turks, and for Christians to exact or permit such self-degradation is not only a shame, but a sin. Have not some of you been in free Serbia, and seen how the schoolchildren behave there?' 'No, none of them.' But at these words they exchanged glances, and began to cheer up a little. They invited us to come into the church, and presently brought thither a man from the village who had been in free Serbia. This man wore a turban, was of uncouth aspect, and otherwise looked like the other rayahs, but he was far more outspoken than the monks. We desired him to say if the Serbian schoolchildren prostrated themselves as these did. 'Of course not,' cried he; 'but then in Serbia *everything* is different. There they have good roads, good judges, peace, and prosperity; here there is nothing but disorder and zulum' (Turk, violence and oppression).

"Prostrations like those of the schoolchildren at Gratchanitza frequently greeted us during this journey, and we cannot think that any civilised traveller would see them with less distress than ourselves. But one's own feeling at thus witnessing the degradation of fellow-creatures and fellow-Christians gives but a faint idea of what is felt by the Serbs of the Principality to whom these rayahs stand in the relation of brethren of race, nay, often are near of kin. Monks, merchants, and emigrants of all sorts, pass constantly from the Turkish ruled districts to free Serbia, and not even the accounts which they give of their position awake such indignation as the involuntary evidence of it afforded by their cringing demeanour, until they learn the manners of a new land."—Pp. 232—3.

A still more distressing illustration of the state of terror in which the Christians live occurred to the travellers at Novi-Bazar. They were lodged by the Turkish authorities in a Christian's house. In order to do them especial honour, the authorities had left three zapties (policemen) in the house to attend upon them. Then, they proceed :—

"They were a terrible nuisance those imperious, rapacious men turned loose in a rayah's dwelling; no part of the lower house was free from their presence; the women had to hide from them, and the young father of the family was ordered about as their slave. We soon perceived that something was amiss by the repressed cringing air of the man, and sent our dragoman to say that we only wanted one zaptié, and would only give backsheeh to one. However, the other two would not stir, so all we could do was to ask the master of the house into our room, and try to reassure him with kind words; but the sound of our voices caused him to shake like a leaf, and to the most indifferent question he would only give a whispered reply."—Pp. 303—4.

Anxious to obtain from this man some information as to the state of the Christian community in Novi-Bazar, they instructed their dragoman to ask him a few questions; but as the zapties were sitting in a room just below, the man was in agonies lest they should hear the travellers talking with him. Before he could be reassured, the ladies had to talk with each other in a loud voice to deceive the zaptiés below, and to cover the whispered conversation between the dragoman and their host, whom they described as "a young man with a fresh colour and rounded contour; an European, but quaking, almost convulsed, with fear."

"The whispers became quicker and more eager. Our question as to the state of the Christians had acted like the sudden withdrawal of the dam from a stream; the pent-up waters overflowed—the rayah was pouring out his tale. 'The Christian community of Novi-Bazar is at the mercy of the Mussulmans; they enter houses both by day and night, take what they choose, and behave as they will. Raise an arm or speak a word, and you bring on yourself death or the loss of a limb. Make a representation to the authorities, and you are ruined by the revenge of those of whom you have dared to complain.'

"We asked if within the last few years things had become better or worse.

"'In so far they are better that the officials now sent from Constantinople are jealous of the beys, and the beys of them, and the two opposing cliques act as some sort of check on each other. The Christians are less persecuted in their dress and other trifles, and they may enter their own quarter of the town on horseback, though it would still not be safe to ride past a Mussulman in the road or the bazaar. On the other hand, since last year great repression has been exercised, for fear of the Christians rising to join the Serbians over the border. We have been obliged to do forced labour in raising defences, and to contribute both in food and money to the maintenance of troops—and such troops! Do you know that last summer *Bashi-Bazouks* were sent to Novi-Bazar? But no insult, no injury is so hard to bear as that of Mussulmans carrying off Christian girls. Lately a maiden of the rayah community was servant in a Mussulman family. Suddenly her parents were informed that she had become a Mohammedan; she was not suffered to return to them nor see them, but was sent off to Saraïevo. She escaped, came back to her family, and they ventured to give her shelter ; but the Mussulmans tracked her home, and their vengeance fell upon the whole Christian community. Out of its 110 houses, at least 100 were in their estimate connected with the escape of the poor girl. All felt the weight of their wrath, and several were completely ruined."—Pp. 305—6.

Speaking of Stara Serbia, or Old Serbia, Miss Mackenzie and Miss Irby say :—

"The condition of affairs is indeed bad enough to reduce to despair all its inhabitants, excepting, of course, those evil men who thrive on it. The Porte having exerted energies sufficient to extinguish national liberty in Albania, and to drive great numbers of Albanians to apostatise, has never carried its pains to the point of bringing its new adherents into the attitude of orderly citizens. Whenever authority is exerted over them, it is in order to obtain recruits, or to impose Turkish officials in lieu of the old hereditary Governors—not to enforce a just treatment of the Christians. In the towns of Stara Serbia the Governor is a Turkish official, sometimes an Osmanli who does not know the language of the country, sometimes an Albanian who has served in the regular army. This official supports his authority by aid of a few zaptiés and cavasses in his own service, and these useful persons derive their pay chiefly from what they can rob from the people. The mudir, kaimakan, or pasha buys his post, to begin with, and is then left to enjoy it so short a time that his chief aim is to re-imburse himself as quickly as possible. Every one knows this, so Mussulmans and Christians alike ply him with bribes. But besides enriching himself, he has to raise the Sultan's taxes. If the Mussulmans will not pay their share, he must doubly fleece the Christians ; for the Mussulmans are not to be trifled with, as, should he offend them, they may bribe some higher authority to remove him from his post. At Prishtina this was constantly the case: the mudir we found there was the second in a year, and before we left the district he was already deposed."—Pp. 255—6.

There are many things in this volume which serve to throw considerable light upon what has puzzled many persons in this country, namely, the announcement that in the great Council recently called to decide on the proposals of the Christian Powers, the heads of the various Christian Churches in the Sultan's dominion gave their vote against those proposals. It appears that all the highest officers in the Greek Church are appointed by the Turkish Government.

"To this day," say the writers, "no prelate throughout the Ottoman empire can exercise his functions without an Imperial firman."—P. 32.

Again, speaking of Stara Serbia, they say :—

"Of the Christian community the principle representative is properly the bishop ; hence nothing could more effectually take the heart out of the Sclavs in Turkey, than the transfer of this important office o Greeks, who do not care a rush for Sclavonic interests. In most parts of Old Serbia the idea we found associated with a bishop was that of a person who carried off what few paras the Turks had left."—P. 258.

Very significant also is the following :—

" Throughout the Serb provinces still under Turkey—Boznia, Herzegovina, and Stara Serbia—we found all the bishops Greeks ; one only was present in his diocese, and he had but lately returned from Constantinople to squeeze from the wretched peasantry that revenue which his compeers where staying in Constantinople to spend. In default of payment, the Turkish authorities are invoked to extort the bishop's dues : and the minor clergy, fleeced by their superiors, are constrained to sell every rite of the Church. One peasant affirmed that the corpse of his brother had been left lying in his house until he could raise what the priest asked to bury it—two gold ducats paid in advance. Throughout the Sclavonic provinces the Greek bishop has become enrolled in the same category as the Turkish Governors ; and, so soon as a million of Serbs secured to themselves autonomous administration, they placed their relations to the œcumenical patriarch on the same footing as their vassalage to the Padishah."—P. 375.

TURKISH RULE IN PALESTINE.

We will now turn to another traveller, whose evidence relates to a different part of the country under Turkish rule. Captain Charles Warren was engaged for several years in making explorations in Syria, and especially at Jerusalem. It is not necessary to dwell on the many obstacles thrown in his way by the disorder prevailing in the country, and the duplicity, trickery, and bad faith of the Turkish authorities. We will merely cite a few passages illustrative of the execrable misrule which smites the land of Palestine with blight and desolation. In a chapter on the " Resources of Palestine," he enume- rates the principal reasons why it is now so unfruitful and unhealthy, and the difficulties in the way of improvement :—

"The first and foremost difficulty is the present bad government; the people are oppressed, are wronged ; there is no feeling of security for property or person, no justice, no honesty, among the officials. Bribery and corruption, according to our meaning of the terms, are mild words to use towards the infamous means by which money is extorted from the poor. And, unfortu- nately, the maladministration commences from the top ; no pasha could afford to be honest, no governor-general could venture to be just. The whole organism of the country lies on a rotten foundation, which is constantly being underpinned by the fortunes and lives of the Christians, and often, too, by those of the Moslems who have not been sufficiently wily to avoid getting into difficulties; but nothing will ever make that rotten foundation solid, based, as it is, on the Turks' view that the Christians and Jews cannot be admitted to an equal position in the country with the followers of the Prophet. The Moslem religion has entered into a phase which will admit of no prosperity in the land. Days were when trade by Christians and Jews was fostered, when the rulers of the country understood the art of governing; but now nothing is taught but the art of misrule, for Moslem fortunes are in the hands of the barbarous Turk. . . . .

"It is not the Christian alone of Syria that the Turk oppresses: the Arab Moslem is, if not equally, yet most hardly used. Many a time have the Arab Moslems said to me, 'When will you take this country and rid us of our oppressors; anything is better than their rule.' For the Turk has no affinity of race or language to connect him with, or give him a right to rule, the Arab. He has no power of sympathising with the Semitic races, and his religion is but in name. The Arab, if I may use such an expression, is a Moslem by nature; the Turk cannot become a Moslem by art.

"He is sent to Palestine to govern badly; he is given but a small salary, and is obliged to squeeze the people in order to pay his own officials and to live, to recoup himself for what he has paid for his appointment in the past, and to carry away with him something for the future wherewith he may buy a higher appointment, or purchase immunity for the consequences of his evil deeds, should complaints be made against his rule.

"The Turk can never govern Palestine well; and until he departs the country must remain half desert, half prison; for it is his policy to leave it so. He wants it to continue impoverished, so that it may not tempt the cupidity of stronger nations. This was brought home to me once, when, in conversation with an eminent Turk, I was pressing the advantages of a bridge across the Jordan and other matters; he answered me warmly, 'We want no discoveries; we want no attention paid to Palestine; we want no roads. Leave the place alone. If it becomes rich, we shall lose it; if it remains poor, it will continue in our hands. God be praised.' In vain I urged that if the country were well governed there would be no occasion for taking it from Turkey. His idea was, 'If we make it valuable, you will want it. Let us keep it in poverty.' Well! he tries to keep it in poverty, and succeeds to some extent in reality, and to a great extent in appearance. . . . .

"The fruit-trees are taxed, even from the day on which they are planted, year by year, though they may not be productive for a long time to come ; so that if a man plants a thousand fig-trees or olives, he pays nearly £10 sterling per annum for years before they yield him any profit. For what purpose can such a system be put in force, except for retarding cultivation, and keeping back the country? It certainly cannot be for the purpose of getting a revenue, for with such a law few will plant.

"The people are treated with equal cruelty in regard to the gathering in of their corn. When they have thrashed and winnowed, they leave it heaped up on the floor for the government inspector to see and take his share ; and often it happens that a large portion is decayed or destroyed before he arrives."— *Underground Jerusalem*, pp. 449—54.

TURKISH RULE IN SYRIA.

"Unexplored Syria" is the title of a work published by Captain Burton, who was for a considerable time British Consul at Damascus.

"Captain Burton," says the reviewer in the *Times*, "is eminently conscientious and accurate in his observations, and he tells us quite enough to confirm us in the idea that the administration of Syria, as of other Turkish provinces, is execrable. So mercilessly have the villagers been oppressed and

fleeced by the tax-gatherers, that for a hundred and fifty years past there has
been a steady exodus from the more settled districts to the remote settlements
that look towards the Euphrates desert. We have the statement that in the
last five years of Raschid Pasha's administration no less than seventeen
mountain villages were depopulated, while in a single autumn between seven
hundred and eight hundred families had taken their flight to the eastward."

"We can hardly wonder," says Captain Burton, "at the exodus when we
are told that nearly half the settlements of the Jaydúr district, the ancient
Jhiræa—eleven out of twenty-four—have been within twelve months ruined by
the usurer and the tax-gatherer. . . . . . It is hardly necessary to dwell
on the short-sighted and miserable management which drives an industrious
peasantry from its hearths and homes to distant settlements, where defence is
much more easy than offence, and where, as Cromwell said of Pease Burn, ten
men to hinder are better than a hundred to make their way. This upon a
small scale is a specimen of the system which keeps down to a million and a
half the population of a province which, though not larger than Lancashire and
Yorkshire united, in the days of Strabo and Josephus supported its ten
millions and more."—Pp. 179—181

We will borrow one other uotation from that portion of "Unexplored Syria " which we owe to Mrs. Burton's pen :—

"From Dinán we resumed our way through the Jibbah Bisherri, the 'village
land of Bisherri,' which lies on the western or seaward face of the Libanus.
This is the heart of the Maronite or purely Christian region ; and this district,
like Jezzin, farther south, and Sadad (the ancient Zedad ?) to the north-east,
produces a manly, independent race, fond of horses and arms, with whom I am
not ashamed to own community of faith.

" Undisturbed by the defiling presence of Rashid Pasha, the people are
happy and contented ; their industry has converted every yard of rock-ledge
into a miniature field ; they show a steadily increasing population, resulting
from the absence of the tax-gatherer and the recruiting officer ; and their only
troubles are those bred and born of Ottoman intrigues, of that barbarous policy
which still says, ' Divide and rule them all.' Long may the Règlement de la
Montagne reign ! may Muscovite lord it in Stamboul ere a Moslem governor is
suffered to rule the land of the Maronite ! The words applied by Dr. Hooker
to Marocco are perfectly descriptive of unhappy Syria under her present
affliction:—'The government is despotic, cruel, and wrong-headed in every
sense ; from the Sultan to the lowest soldier, all are paid by squeezing those in
their power.

" Marocco itself is more than half ruinous, and its prisons loaded ; the
population of the whole kingdom is diminishing ; and what with droughts,
locusts, cholera, and prohibitory effects of the most arbitrary description, the
nation is on the brink of ruin ; and but that two-thirds of the kingdon is independent of the Sultan's authority, being held by absolute mountain chiefs, who
defy his power to tax or interfere with them, and that the European merchants
maintain the coast trade, and the consuls keep the Sultan's emissaries in check,
Marocco would present a scene of the wildest disorder."—*Unexplored Syria*,
pp. 108, 109.

Turkish Rule in Bulgaria.

Mr. Henry C. Barkley is a gentleman who has been engaged for many years in connection with railway work in Turkey. In his work recently published, entitled, "Between the Danube and Black Sea," he records principally his experiences in Bulgaria. Of the Bulgarians he speaks in terms of commendation as a quiet, industrious, honest people; but, like all other travellers, he testifies to the cruel and oppressive character of Turkish rule. He says:—

"The Bulgarians, and also the Turkish villagers, are loud in their complaints of the injustice and tyranny of the Turkish officials. All—from the governor-general to the hangman—think it right and just, when on a journey, to quarter themselves on the peasants, without ever thinking of paying; and at the same time they demand the services of their host and his family, and the best of everything there is to be had. The largest and most prosperous of the villages are built as far as possible from the main roads leading to and from the fortified towns, such as Widdin, Rustchuk, Shumla, &c. If they are on the line of march, the troops live on them at free quarters, their carts and beasts are seized for transport services, and the owners themselves forced to accompany them as drivers, and are obliged to find food for themselves and fodder for the cattle, for all of which they receive no recompence. In consequence of this, all the villages that, from force of circumstances, have to be near some main road, are a miserable collection of hovels offering but small temptation to the traveller. About twelve miles from Varna, and not far off the route to Shumla, is the flourishing village of Gebedgi, which is partly Turkish, partly Bulgar. On entering it one is at once struck by the appearance of prosperity exhibited in the well-built houses and large flocks of cattle. Between this village and the road is a swamp with a narrow but deep brook running through it. To assist in the construction of the line which passed by the village, I caused a road to be made across the marsh, and a wooden bridge thrown over the brook. The first night after the bridge was completed it was cut down; and on making inquiries about it, a Turk told me that, rather than live with this easy access to the road, the inhabitants, both Turks and Bulgars, would burn their houses and migrate to some spot where Turkish officials, Turkish troops, and above all Turkish zaptiehs, could not so easily get at them. 'Above all, zaptiehs,' for they are the constant and never-ending curse of all the villages, whether Turkish or Bulgar. They are recruited from the very lowest and most ruffianly of the Turks. Many, if not most, of them have been brigands, and all are robbers. Their pay (even when they get it) is not sufficient to support them, and therefore they depend on their *position* to secure the comforts of life. They *live* on the peasants, and all they have, from their pipe to their horse, has been robbed from them. Over and over again I have seen every woman and girl of an entire Christian village disappear as if by magic at the approach of a zaptieh; and when he enters the village, all the men stand staring about, watching to see what may take place, like a flock of sheep when a strange dog comes among them."—Preface, pp. vi.—viii.

Mr. Barkley first went to Bulgaria soon after the conclusion of the Crimean war. One of his earliest insights into the character of Turkish rule is given in the following passage. Speaking of the town of Rustindju, Mr. Barkley says :—

"We had a visit from the Tchorbadjie, or head man of the little town. He was a Bulgar, as were nearly all the inhabitants, and proved a quiet, decent fellow. There was a dash of melancholy in his looks, which we thought was accounted for when he told us that when the war first broke out a regiment of Bashi-Bazouks was sent up here to look after a few Cossacks who had crossed the Danube, and were acting as scouts. They encamped for the night on the very spot we were just quitting, and before they left the next morning they set fire to the town, and even took the corn out of the granary, piled it up in the streets, and burnt it. Some of the young Bulgars remonstrated with them, and were at once cut down and hacked to pieces. Of the horrors the women went through I dare not write ; but of one thing I feel sure—as long as there is a Sultan in Turkey every Bulgar will curse him for having let loose such a mob of devils on them. We afterwards heard this tale corroborated by many Christians and a few Turks, though the latter tried to make the best of it."—Pp. 18, 19.

Speaking of the intense cold which occasionally prevails in that country, Mr. Barkely tells the following anecdote :—

"The Pasha of Varna had some time before this sent orders to a distant village for a supply of wood. Five arabas, each with a Bulgar driver, arrived at dusk, just as the storm commenced. They inquired where they should deliver the wood, but no one knew exactly where the woodstack had better be made, and the pasha's servants, fearing if it were discharged at the wrong place that they should have to remove it themselves, determined to do nothing till the morning. The arabas were therefore escorted into a large barrack-yard surrounded with high walls, and there locked in for the night. The cries and shouts for help from the five men were disregarded, and no further notice was taken of them till the next morning, when they were found huddled together in the snow, all dead. No matter ; they were Bulgar dogs, and it was Kisnet ! No one was punished ; the wood was not paid for ; but pay-ment for the keep of the wretched bullocks was extorted from the friends of the dead men when they came to fetch them away a month later. Look out, 'sick man !' you are getting weaker every day, and these 'dogs' are waxing stronger ; they will turn and worry you before long, and, when that day comes, who will care to drive them from their lawful prey ?"—Pp. 62, 63.

We come now to another most intelligent traveller, Mr. Arthur J. Evans. His experience brings down our knowledge of the state of things in the European provinces of Turkey to the most recent date. While he and his brother were travelling through Boznia and the Herzegovina, the insurrection actually broke out. In what they saw and heard of the universally oppressed condition of the people, there is ample cause for the insurrection, without having recourse to the idea of foreign instigation. "The wrongs of the Christians in Boznia," says Mr. Evans, "have been intolerable ;" and few who read his volume will doubt the justice of the remark. Here is one extrac illustrative of those intolerable wrongs :—

"Aug. 22.—To-day we made the acquaintance of the German Consul, Count Von Bothmar, who expressed considerable surprise at our arriving here unmolested. From him and the other members of the consular body, who were very ready to supply us with full details as to the stirring events that are taking place around us, we learnt many interesting facts relative to the causes and course of the insurrection in Bosnia. These accounts, and others from trustworthy sources, reveal such frantic oppressions and gross misgovernment as must be hardly credible to Englishmen. We have heard all that can be said on the Turkish side, but the main facts remain unshaken.

"The truth is, that outside Serajevo and a few of the larger towns where there are Consuls or 'resident Europeans,' neither the honour, property, nor the lives of Christians are safe. Gross outrages against the person—murder itself—can be committed in the rural districts with impunity. The authorities are blind; and it is quite a common thing for the gendarmes to let the perpetrator of the grossest outrage, if a Mussulman, escape before their eyes. Miss Irby, who has made many inquiries on these subjects, estimates that in the Medgliss, the only court where Christian evidence is even legally admitted, 'the evidence of twenty Christians would be outweighed by two Mussulmans.' But why, it may be asked, do not the Christians appeal to the Consuls for protection? In the first place, in a mountainous country like Bosnia, with little means of communication, to do so would in most cases be a physical impossibility. In the second place, as Count Bothmar assured us, if such complaint is made to a Consul, so surely is the complaining rayah more cruelly oppressed than before; nor is consular authority so omnipresent as to save him and his family from ruin. 'God alone knows,' he exclaimed, 'what the rayahs suffer in the country districts!' Remembering the revolting scenes, of which I had been a witness, at the Christian gathering near Comusina, I could believe this.

"But the most galling oppression, and the main cause of the present revolt, is to be found in the system and manner of taxation. The centralised government, set up in Bosnia since 1851, is so much machinery for wringing the uttermost farthing out of the unhappy Bosniac rayah. The desperate efforts of Turkish financiers, on the eve of national bankruptcy, have at last made the burden of taxation more than even the long-suffering Bosniac can bear. It was the last straw.

"The principal tax—besides the house and land tax, and that paid by the 'Christian,' in lieu of military service, which is wrung from the poorest rayah for every male of his family down to the baby in arms—is the eighth, or, as it is facetiously called by the tax-collector, the tenth, which is levied on all produce of the earth. With regard to the exaction of this tax, every conceivable iniquity is practised. To begin with, its collection is farmed out to middle-men, and these *ex officio* pitiless, are usually by origin the scum of the Levant. The Osmanli or the Sclavonic Mahometan possesses a natural dignity and self-respect which disinclines him for such dirty work. The men who come forward and offer the highest price for the license of extortion are more often Christians—Fanariote Greeks—adventurers from Stamboul, members of a race perhaps the vilest of mankind. No considerations of honour, or religion, or humanity, restrain these wretches. Having acquired the right to farm the taxes of a given district, the Turkish officials and gendarmerie are bound to support them in wringing the uttermost farthing out of the *misera contribuens plebs,* and it is natural that this help should be most readily forthcoming when needed to break the resistance of the rayah.

"These men time their visitation well. They appear in the villages before the harvest is gathered, and assess the value of the crops according to the present prices, which, of course, are far higher just before the harvest than after it. But the rayahs would be well contented if their exactions stopped here. They possess, however, a terrible lever for putting the screw on the miserable tiller. The harvest may not be gathered till the tax, which is pitilessly levied in cash, has been extorted. If the full amount—and they often double or treble the legal sum—is not forthcoming, the tax-gatherer simply has to say—'Then your harvest shall rot on the ground till you pay it !' And the rayah must see the produce of his toil lost, or pay a ruinous imposition, which more than swamps his profits. Or, if he still remains obstinate, there are other paraphernalia of torture worthy of the vaults of the Inquisition. A village will occasionally band together to defend themselves from these extortioners. Thereupon the tithe-farmer applies to the civil power, protesting that if he does not get the full amount from the village, he will be unable in his turn to pay the Government. The zaptiehs, the factotums of the Turkish officials, are immediately quartered on the villagers, and live on them, insult their wives, and ill-treat their children. With the aid of these gentry, all kinds of personal tortures are applied to the recalcitrant. In the heat of summer men are stripped naked and tied to a tree, smeared over with honey or other sweet stuff, and left to the tender mercies of the insect-world. For winter extortion it is found convenient to bind people to stakes, and leave them barefooted to be frostbitten ; or at other times they are shoved into a pigstye, and cold water poured on them. A favourite plan is to drive a party of rayahs up a tree, or into a chamber, and then smoke them with green wood. Instances are recorded of Bosniac peasants being buried up to their heads in earth, and left to repent at leisure. I will quote a single instance of these practices, communicated by the Princess Julia of Servia to the author of 'Servia and the Servians :'—'A poor woman, frantic with agony, burst into the palace of the princess at Belgrade. She had been assessed by the Turkish authorities of a village in Bosnia of a sum which she had no means of paying. . . . . *She was smoked.* This failed of extracting the gold. She begged for a remission, and stated her inability to pay. In answer, she was tossed into the river Drina, and after her were thrown her two infant children—one of four years old, the other of two. Before her eyes, notwithstanding her frantic efforts to save them, her children perished. Half-drowned and insensible, she was dragged to land by a Servian peasant. She made her way to Belgrade, believing, from the character of the princess for humanity, that she would aid her. Of course, to do so was out of the question.'

"Gustave Thoemmel, who was attached to the American Consulate here, relates how the application of such tortures drove many Bosnian rayahs to desperation in 1865. No less than 500 families took refuge across the borders from these inquisitors in the spring of that year. They were, however, turned back, and forced to return to their homes in Bosnia in a most deplorable state. 'Complaint,' says Thoemmel, 'about outrages of this kind are scarcely ever brought forward, since the rayah seldom obtains evidence, or even hearing, and his complaining only brings down on him increased persecution ; so it happens that the higher officials often remain in ignorance of the barbarities . perpetrated by their underlings.' "—Pp. 254—9.

Mr. J. Evans gives instances which came within his own observation of the brutal insolence with which the officials of the Mahommedan Government deal with the Christian Bosniacs when not under the immediate surveillance of foreign Consuls.

" Briefly," he says, " they treated them like a herd of cattle ; and it is hard to say which was the more revolting—the intolerable insolence or the downright cruelty. I was standing," he continues, " in one of the circles where a Bosnian gleeman was rehearsing a national epic, when the spell of the song was rudely broken by a zaptieh, who, bursting through the ring of listeners, and thrusting the rayahs to right and left, stood before the embers in the middle, and playing with his cutlass in one hand, demanded who would light his pipe in such a savage tone as quite infuriated me. The Bosniacs took it more calmly. The old minstrel laid down his lute, and paused for awhile in his lay. For a few moments there was a moody silence, as if some blunted sense of injury had outlived long use of wrong ; then a fine man stepped forward sheepishly and lit the bully's pipe.

"Another time a knot of peasants were gathered together in friendly converse on the grassy middle-lane, when two zaptiehs rushed forward with whips and flogged them away, *women* as well as men ! But the worst instance of brutality that came within my observation took place while I was discussing a bottle of Slavonian wine, and exchanging English songs for Bosnian, with a merry group of rayahs belonging mostly to the Greek Church—'Serbs,' as they proudly called themselves—who had come to take part in the fair and festa of their Roman Catholic rivals. Of a sudden our festivities were broken in upon by the sounds of a scuffle behind, accompanied by such shrieks as made me start up ; and the firelight fell upon a gendarme—the same, I think, who had interrupted the minstrelsy—who with a stick or some kind of weapon was beating an old Christian man as if he were a pig, and kicking the poor cringing wretch the while till he howled for mercy. I was stepping forward to interpose, but two Bosniacs clutched hold of me and held me back, whispering, with more covered hatred than can be described, ' 'Tis only the Turks !' The zaptieh, however, not wishing to provoke Frankish intervention, desisted from his belabouring, and left his victim to limp away as best he might. The group of ' Serbs ' had not shown any sign of attempting a rescue, but I saw more than one brow ominously knit for the moment. But the visible emotion was transient, and their faces relapsed into that impassable stolidity which is the normal expression of the Bosnian rayah."—Pp. 141—3.

And now we close with the testimony of the last traveller who has visited Turkey—Sir George Campbell. Personally he is more favourably disposed to the Turkish race than most of those who have dwelt long among them. The more important, therefore, is the evidence he gives as to the execrable character of their government :—

" When," he says, " we come to political rights and trusts, then I say that, at this moment, and now perhaps more than at any previous period of Turkish history, the Christians are placed in a humiliating and enthralled position which has no parallel in the world. Think of a system under which no Christian can bear arms in any capacity, not even the bâton of a policeman, nor exercise any executive authority, even the pettiest ; under which not only the whole army, but the whole executive administration—the whole police down to the village watchman—are all of the dominant Mahommedan minority, while the Christian majority are entirely and without exception a subject people ! Compare this state of things with the liberal government of the Mogul Emperors in India, where the Hindoos were employed in thousands and tens of thousands, both in the army and the civil administration, where many of the chief ministers were Hindoos, and where one of the Emperors even went so far as to appoint a Hindoo General to be Governor of Mahommedan Cabul. Compare it with the everyday and uncoerced practices of native States in India at this day. There is hardly a Hindoo State which has not many Mahommedans in its higher offices, and hardly a Mahommedan State which has not many Hindoos in similar offices.

"Whatever, then, the material position of the Christians of Turkey, and however their sufferings from bad government may be, more or less, in particular provinces and under particular Pashas, it seems to me that they have everywhere a political grievance of the most crying and outrageous description. For the rest, it cannot be doubted there is overwhelming concurrence of testimony to this : that under a most inefficient and corrupt Government, and the extreme domination of an alien race, Christians were very frequently ill-treated and oppressed in an extreme degree. It is patent that they were often outraged by Turks, and plundered by Circassians. Yet on the whole, considering the extreme badness of the situation, the excessive opportunities to impune outrage and oppression in the hands of a race themselves ill-used, discontented, and downgoing, the irritation natural to the attempt to cure one evil by another— the domination of the Turks by the abuses of ill-regulated Consular protection —looking to all the circumstances, I must say, I think the wonder is, not that there was so much outrage and plunder, but that there was not more. It is only because the Turks are not personally a very bad race that the case was not worse. But things were coming to a crisis. The tension between the races was increasing. The pot of discontent, oppression, and recrimination was ready to boil over."—*A Recent View of Turkey*, Sir George Campbell, p. 112.

It would be easy to multiply these testimonies; the difficulty, indeed, is where to stop. We had once thought of subjoining to these recent evidences of Turkish misrule taken from travellers a series of extracts from more recent Consular reports, and other official documents to the same effect. But this has been already so well done by the Rev. W. Denton, in his admirable little volume entitled "The Christians of Turkey," that we must be content to refer our readers to his pages, where they will find also abundant other matter illustrative of the same subject.

www.ingramcontent.com/pod-product-compliance
Lightning Source LLC
Chambersburg PA
CBHW021431090426
42739CB00009B/1440